Walks in A

CW00524972

Clan Walk Guides

Walks in
Argyll and Bute

Mary Welsh
and
Christine Isherwood

First Published by Clan Books 2003

ISBN 1 873597 18 5

Text and Illustrations
© Mary Welsh
and
Christine Isherwood
2003

The authors wish to express their gratitude to VisitScotland for their enthusiastic and positive assistance during the groundwork for this volume; also to Jennifer Outhwaite for her help and support.

Clan Books
Clandon House
The Cross, Doune
Perthshire
FK16 6BE

Printed by
Cordfall Ltd, Glasgow

Red deer

C.M.Isherwood

Authors' Note

Please remember on all these walks:

Wear suitable clothes and take adequate waterproofs.

Walk in strong footwear; walking boots are advisable.

Carry the relevant map and know how to use it.

Take extra food and drink as emergency rations.

Carry a whistle; remember six long blasts repeated at one minute intervals is the distress signal.

Do not walk alone, and tell someone where you are going.

If mist descends, return.

Keep all dogs under strict control. Observe all 'No Dogs' notices— they are there for very good reasons.

Readers are advised that while the authors have taken every effort to ensure the accuracy of this guidebook, changes can occur after publication. You should check locally on transport, accommodation, etc. The publisher would welcome notes of any changes. Neither the publisher nor the authors can accept responsibility for errors, omissions or any loss or injury.

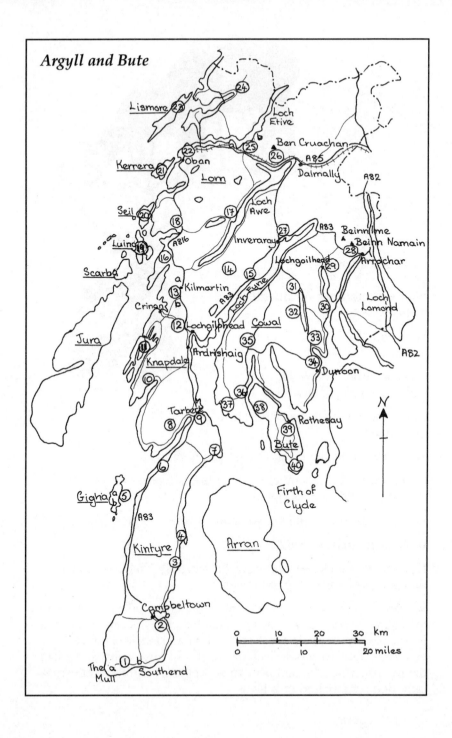

Argyll and Bute

Contents

contents continued page 6

Lighthouse and foghorn on the Mull, Kintyre

Park in the Gap parking area, grid ref. 598081, just before the gate to the road to the lighthouse.

The **lighthouse,** operational in 1788, was built by the Trustees for Northern lighthouses. It stands on the sheer cliffs of the Mull, its light a warning to shipping to keep well away from the great turbulence and notorious currents around this southerly tip of Kintyre. Access to the lighthouse is by a long, steeply descending, narrow road and, by the last hair-pin bend stands a cottage, Ballinamoil, where, before the lighthouse was built, a shepherd kept a lamp burning to warn sailors of the dangers.

On 2 June 1994 a **Chinook helicopter**, carrying military and civilian anti-terrorist experts, crashed in thick mist, into the hillside high above the lighthouse. They were on their way from Northern Ireland to a conference in Inverness-shire. All were killed. A sturdy cairn on the hillside is a memorial to this tragic disaster.

Lighthouse, Mull of Kintyre

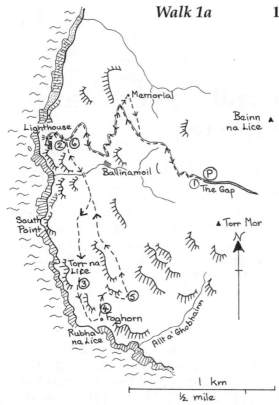

Walk 1a

1. Go through the gap beside the padlocked gate and begin your descent of the very steep, twisting, narrow road. It drops down between heather and then bracken and from it you can spot the lighthouse on its promontory. You might also glimpse Antrim and Rathlin Island, which lie 12 miles across the Irish Sea. Look also for gannets as they fly fast, just above the waves—brilliantly white birds, with black-tipped wings. Pass the helicopter pad and go on down to the lighthouse to enjoy the views.

2. Return to the helicopter pad. Here turn right along a widish grassy trod, with a fence to your left. Take note of the warning on a board that you must cover your ears if the foghorn sounds. Then the track leads to a gate in the wall ahead, through which you pass. Beyond, begin your descent of a long flight of steps, with a rail on the sea side, followed by a railed grassy path. The lovely way continues with alternating railed steps and railed paths along the dramatic cliffs, with superb views out to sea and far down to the rocky shore below.

3. Go past a hillock to the right, where you can see the remains of a 1914–18 wartime signalling station. Finally the railed way climbs to the white building which houses the foghorn. Behind the locked building is a flat grassy area, where in autumn sheep's bit flowers. From here Ireland seems very close and it isn't difficult to imagine St Columba wanting to bring his Christian message over the short stretch of water.

4. With your back to the sea and the foghorn, walk inland on a clear stony way, climbing uphill. Follow it as it winds steadily left below a huge cliff, where you might spot roe deer. Continue on to join a widish track and climb right. You are now on the route taken by vehicles used by the farmer and those maintaining the foghorn. This brings you to a sheltered hollow in the hills.

Gannets

5. Then the way winds and climbs gently left, and is well marked by vehicle wheels. To the right steep bracken-clad slopes rear up toward crags. Walk on the wide level way where dwarf willow grows underfoot. The path goes on through a vast area of heather. Look here for pockets of long grass, flattened by resting deer. Then the lighthouse and the wall passed through at the outset come into view. Keep on the high-level way to go through a gap in the wall, close by a sheep pen. Beyond, turn half left to pass the warning board seen earlier. Descend steadily, converging with the fence, to pass through a gap in it and walk on to the road.

6. Turn right and begin the long climb towards the car park. When about two-thirds of the way, look left and upwards towards the commemorative cairn to the helicopter disaster. To visit the site of the crash, take a clear path on the left, just beyond the next hairpin bend. If you miss this path there are several more, leaving the road, further up. All will take you across the rough moorland to the memorial. Look down on the superb view, then take the left of three paths to return to the road. Turn left and continue to the parking area.

Practicals

Type of walk: With the railed fences and paths in place for nearly a mile this is a very safe path from which to enjoy a dramatic cliff walk along Argyll's nearest point to Ireland. The return through the hills is delightful.

Distance: 4 miles/6.5km
Time: 2–3 hours
Map: OS Explorer 356

Southend—
St Columba's Footprints and Dunaverty Castle, Kintyre

Park in the Keil car park, grid ref. 671077, on the north side of the B842, west of the village of Southend.

The barren hills and sheer cliffs of the Mull of Kintyre give way to grassy slopes, flats and long sandy beaches at **Southend** where the village has developed as a small resort. The sandy bays are sheltered by the Mull and swimming is safe. Here too, seals swim, cavort and lie out on rocks to the east of Keil Point. Otters dive and frolic after fish, just off the rocky ribs that run out into the sea. Close to the car park is a sign directing you up steps to a hillock, to see two footprints carved in the summit rock. One is known to be the work of a 19th century stonemason, the other is ancient and perhaps was used in the inauguration of kings, who would promise to follow in the footsteps of their ancestors, (see 'carved footprint of fealty', walk 13b Dunadd Hill).

The very scant remains of **Dunaverty Castle** stand on a precipitous headland at the far end of Dunaverty Bay. In 1647 the remnants of the defeated royalist MacDonald's army, after the battle

Dunaverty Rock

of Rhunahaorine Moss, surrendered the castle after a siege during which their drinking water ran out. Instead of being honourably taken prisoner they were murdered, many being cast off the cliffs to die on the rocks far below. The murderers were the Covenanters, under the command of General David Leslie, who was advised to do this by his chaplain.

Walk 1b

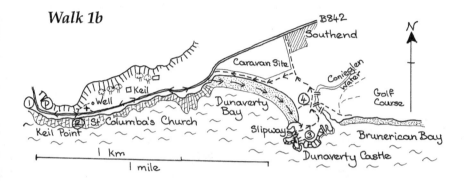

1. Leave the car park and cross the road to stand by the low sea wall from where you might spot seals and otters. Cross back and walk towards the village to come to a signpost directing you up steps to see St Columba's footprints. From the foot of the rocky knoll you can walk left to see the caves in the magnificent cliffs and right to see an ancient well. Return to the shore road and walk on to visit St Columba's Chapel. The medieval church was probably built around the 1320s. Look for the many grave-slabs and fragments that lie inside the roofless church and in the large graveyard.

2. Return to the road and continue on to pass the once rather fine boys' school and then the 'skeleton' of Keil Hotel. Further on you reach the toilet block at the near end of the bay. Pass to the left of the building and go on along the pleasing sands. If the tide is high and you cannot reach the road at the far end, climb the path on to the dunes and continue on. Wind right to pass the old lifeboat station and on towards its disused launching ramp. Cross left over a small concrete barrier, which straddles a narrow sea inlet, and climb the slope opposite. Follow the clear path up the rock slope, with care, and go on up a gully, with firm stone steps to a natural rock balustrade. From here the view is stunning. As you go look for a small fragment of stone wall—all that remains of the castle.

3. Return from the summit and back past the old lifeboat station and continue ahead. Walk the good track with the golf links to your left and the surging Conieglen Water to the right. If you wish to extend your walk along Brunerican Bay, cross the burn by the second bridge and turn right to walk the sands to the shore.

4. On your way back to the car park, follow the track over the golf links to a fence and then head back to the shore. Return to the car park by the same route.

Gulls

Practicals

Type of walk: After some road walking the route continues along a pleasing sandy bay, with the possibility of a sandy extension. The climb up to the top of the headland requires care. There are many historical and archaeological treasures to see and explore. Allow yourself plenty of time.

Distance: 2–3 miles/3.4–4.8km
Time: 2–3 hours
Map: OS Explorer 356

2

Island of Davaar and the old road, Glenramskill, Kintyre

Park in a wide unsignposted lay-by at the start of the shingle causeway, grid ref. 745195. This lies two miles south of Campbeltown. To reach the lay-by follow the narrow road (known locally as the Leerside road) that runs south on the west side of Campbeltown Loch.

Davaar Island sits squarely in between the mouth of Campbeltown Loch and Kildalloig Bay, its bulk giving protection to the harbour at Campbeltown. It is reached by walkers and vehicles by a tidal shingle and sand bar, nearly a mile long, known as the Doirlinn. It is fully exposed at low tide and completely covered when the tide—which comes in fast—is full. Call at the Tourist Information Centre (tel. 01880 820429) at Campbeltown to obtain tide tables, before attempting your walk across the causeway. Allow yourself ample time to cross and return safely— usually 3 hours before and 3 hours after low tide is safe.

Painting, Davaar

In the **seventh cave** along the south shore of Davaar is the famous, inspirational painting of a life size figure of Christ on the Cross. It was painted by Archibald MacKinnon, a local artist, who completed it in secrecy. It was discovered by fishermen in 1887 and every effort was made to find out how it came to be there. Eventually the artist declared himself and confirmed this by showing photographs of himself at work. Sadly the local newspaper reviled the painting and described the artist as egotistical and vain. But things change and in 1934, at the age of 84, Archibald returned from England to a civic welcome and to restore his by now celebrated work. Since his death in the following year the painting has been restored several times.

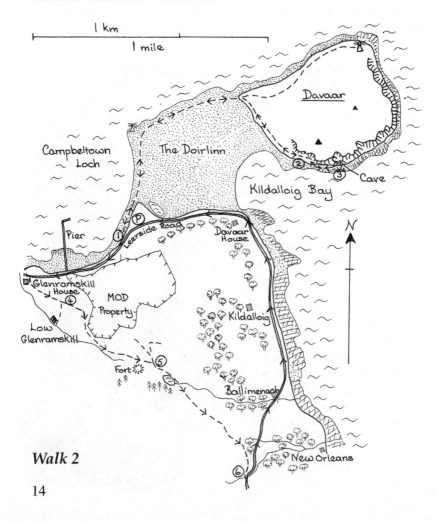

Walk 2

1. From the lay-by walk back a few steps towards Campbeltown to take a gate onto the shingle beach and the continuing shingle bank. Carry on where it widens, passing right of a harbour light. Follow it where it begins to bear right and becomes sandy and much easier to walk. Press on until you reach the island. Climb up a low grassy bank and turn right to dawdle the pleasing, sheep-cropped turf. At a ruined croft the easy way ends.

2. Continue on over a tumble of rocks keeping, where possible, to patches of smaller stone and pebbles. Take time as you progress as the jagged rocks can be slippery and ankle wrenching. If you see a peregrine or a kestrel overhead, stop to observe. Soon you are able to hug the foot of the towering cliffs and this helps progress. After passing several caves, half a mile from the ruined croft, you reach three large caves very close together. The next cave has a sign directing you inside to see the painting. You can discern it without a torch especially if the sun is in the right position but much better to take one with you.

3. Make your return by the same route. On reaching the gate onto the shoreside road, turn right to walk the Leerside road, or the beach, in the direction of Campbeltown. Go past the Ministry of Defence (MOD) jetty and its refuelling station. Carry on until you reach a cart track, on the left side of the road, just before Glenramskill House. Beyond the wall end of the house, climb steadily, with the pretty Glenramskill Burn down to the right. Look right up the valley towards the slopes of Beinn Ghuilean then carry on up the red sandstone track.

4. Where the track swings right to Low Glenramskill farm, go ahead to pass through a gate. Press on uphill, between gorse bushes, with the MOD fence away to your left. Take the short cut to the right before you reach the fence at the point where it bears right. Continue on the

Peregrine

track as it moves steadily right and then winds left to a gate tied to a hurdle. Beyond, a pleasing track ascends a narrow, sheltered, remote valley, with steep grass and heather slopes on either side. A tiny tributary stream of the burn hurries downhill beside you. Pause before you reach the next gate to look right to see a heathery mound, the site of a hill fort. It is a strategic place to establish one on the col between the coast and Campbeltown Loch. Climb the stile beside the gate and join a clear track, the old road.

5. Turn right and go on to pass a pretty loch (reservoir), with conifers and deciduous trees about it. Ford the shallow outflow and continue on the lovely level way. Pass through a gate and look left for a fine view over flowering gorse and then Kildalloig Bay to Davaar Island, where you can see the cairn on top of the sheer cliffs. Use your binoculars to locate the cave visited earlier. Look ahead to see the bold stark cliffs of Achinhoan Head. Stroll on as the way begins to descend, with heather moorland stretching away to the right and pleasing rolling grassland and tree-clad valleys to the left. Continue to the quiet Leerside road.

6. Turn left and stroll through the pleasing countryside to come beside the shore. Idle on, with a lichen-clad wall between you and the beach. Look for eiders, shags, wigeon and mergansers just offshore and curlews, oystercatchers, ringed plovers and turnstones busy ahead of the tide. Follow the road back to the parking lay-by.

Practicals

Type of walk: An exciting, challenging walk to see the cave painting on Davaar. The route over the hill and the return by the shore road rounds off a very good ramble.

Distance: 6 miles/9.8km
Time: 3–4 hours
Map: OS Explorer 356

3

Saddell Castle, Bay and Abbey, Kintyre

Park in the parking area at the beginning of the entrance drive to Saddell Castle, grid ref. 786319. This lies on the south side of the B842 on the south-east side of the tiny village of Saddell.

Saddell Castle is an early 16th century tower-house, surrounded by late 18th century outbuildings. Fragments of the original castle wall survive and are incorporated into the farm buildings. By 1650 the castle was owned by the Campbells. Just over a century later the local lairds decided the castle was too old-fashioned and cold to live in and they built themselves nearby Saddell House. The castle deteriorated and by 1970 it was derelict. In 1976 the Landmark Trust bought the castle, the house and the cottages, on the shore, and restored them for holiday accommodation though none of the buildings is open to the general public.

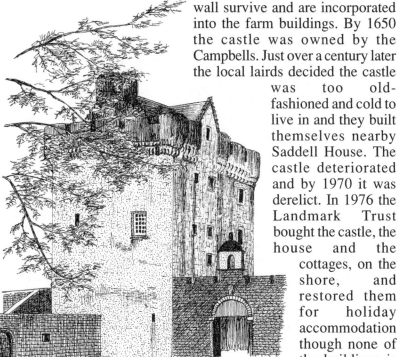

Saddell Castle

17

Saddell Abbey is believed to have been founded around 1148 by Somerled, Lord of the Isles, the Hebridean warrior who defeated the Norse. The tranquil beauty of the 'sandy dale' made it the perfect site for a Cistercian house—far from worldly temptations. By the beginning of the 16th century the Scottish king, James IV, received permission from the Pope to suppress the monastic community. He then gave the abbey lands to the Bishop of Argyll, who built the castle overlooking Kilbrannan Sound. Today little remains of the abbey but at the time of writing scaffolding is in place and work is progressing to stabilise what is left. At the entrance to the abbey, foundations are ready for the building of an interpretative centre to house the many magnificently carved grave slabs and other artefacts.

Walk 3

1. From the parking area pass through the fine wrought iron gates to walk the glorious track, lined with lichen-clad sycamore, oak and lime, with a welcome sign to walkers from the Landmark Trust. Continue down the avenue to the castle. Go through an arch to the right of the outbuildings and on along the track to pass two white houses. Then continue along the shore, where lush vegetation comes right down to the edge of the beach. If the tide is out wander among the 'tortured' rocks. Here you might see a heron feeding and perhaps grey wagtails chasing flies along the seaweed-clad shore.

2. Return past the castle and turn right along a track to cross the bridge over Saddell Water. Carry on to the end of a low wall. Go down steps, on the right, to walk a wonderfully green track that runs

parallel with the shore of Saddell Bay. To the left, and almost completely screened by trees, stands Saddell House. Walk on around the pleasing curving bay. If you have time explore the shore out to Pluck Point.

3. Return along the shore track and turn right to walk the avenue to the B-road. Descend, right, to the village and take a left turn, signed for Saddell Abbey. Bear left at a Y-junction and carry on along the lane to a gate into the graveyard of the Abbey to begin a delightful walk around the precincts.

Pair of grey wagtails

Practicals

Type of walk: Very short but with much to see, together with a delectable stroll along the shore of Saddell Bay.

Distance: 1 ½ miles/2.5km
Time: 1 ½ hours
Map: OS Explorer 356

4

Carradale, Kintyre

Park in the Forest Enterprise Port na Storm car park, grid ref.
811384. This lies on the edge of the village of Carradale, to the left
of the B879, the approach road.

Carradale was once a busy fishing village and popular holiday
destination served by the Clyde steamers. There is still a small
fleet but more recently forestry has had a strong influence on the
village, with large-scale afforestation beginning in the early 1950s.
The history of the village is illustrated at the Network Centre which
is open from Easter to October.

Carradale Bay

1. Turn left out of the car park, following the sign for Deer Hill walk.
   Bear right at the T-junction and go on past a football pitch. Beyond
   it, watch for the easily-missed waymarked (blue post with a red
   footprint) left turn, which climbs steadily. The very pleasant way
   goes on through heather, with many spectacular views of the Arran

Walk 4

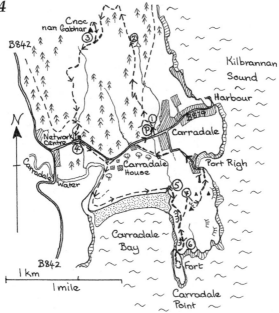

mountains and higher up, of Ailsa Craig. The way then levels at a deer gate. Go through two more deer gates and look for the narrow path, on your right, leading to a tiny dammed pool.

2. Return to the main path and continue, where in summer beautiful St John's wort flowers along the verge. To the left, tall conifers have vast clumps of moss cushioning their roots. Pass through an open area where you might see stonechats perched on the top of bracken fronds. Follow the track as it winds left and climbs steeply again after a tight zig-zag. Look down on Carradale and then over the sea to Galloway. Once you have reached the brow the path winds left, levelling out on high moorland. Take the waymarked track that climbs right. It takes you quite steeply uphill and then winds left to the white-painted trig point on Cnoc nan Gabhar. (Deer Hill) The view is stunning and you will want to linger.

3. Descend the same way to rejoin the main path and walk on (right). Then it descends gently, with heather moorland to the right, and you can look ahead along the coast of Kintyre. After more winding, climbing and then levelling out, the way finally begins its delightful, long, steep descent to join a forest road, where you turn left. After crossing a burn take a path on the right, signposted 'Network Centre', into the forest, where you will enjoy passing below the sweet smelling western hemlock. Just before a stiled fence descend, on the right, two flights of steps to the centre where you might wish to spend time looking at the exhibition and visiting the cafe.

4. Join the road, cross and walk left. Take a track going ahead on the right, keeping parallel with the road. Ignore all side turns and at a triangular junction, follow the way as it winds right. Walk on along the pleasant track with the Carradale Water to your right. Ignore the left turn into the caravan site and carry on to the wonderful sands of Carradale Bay. Pause on the beach to watch common seals—as interested in you as you are in them. Walk east along the sandy bay or, stride the track running behind it. The latter is stiled and ends in sand dunes, where you climb a stile over the fence on to the beach. Follow the narrow path, on the sea side of the fence, to the end of the beach, keeping close beside a hedge on the left and the Allt a' Choinhid to the right, which you cross on a footbridge.

5. Beyond, turn right and continue on a good track through gorse to an area where people park their cars. Cross behind the beach, winding left and then right, aiming for a gate with a white notice on it which says 'no dogs'. By the gate there is a fence and a wall coming in on the left and a wall of a ruin on the right. Climb the stile over the fence, turn right and, after a few steps, follow a good path, left, which carries on uphill to the right of a rocky knoll. Press on along the clear path, through bracken, and then along a short exposed ledge overlooking the bay. On contorted rocks below cormorants idle and oystercatchers preen in a little bay. Soon the path climbs right onto a short heather-clad ridge and the views across the bay and the continuing coastline are superb. Look down on the rocks below to see if there are any seals hauled out.

Common seal

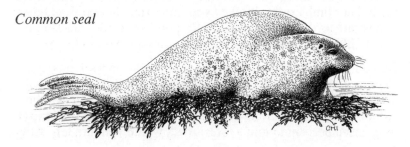

6. Follow the path as it descends, steeply at first, and carries on between small crags. It then swings right to come to the shore. If the tide is out you can cross the sand to walk uphill on a distinct path to Carradale Point, with its superb view and vitrified fort, one of the best in Kintyre. Return the same way, pausing to look across the valley to slopes on your right, where you might spot white wild goats. Press on to the start of the exposed ledge taken earlier. Here leave the path and head right along a narrow animal track, which continues through scattered rhododendrons to a shallow grassy sward. Turn left to continue on grass to a largish open area.

7. Cross this to take a grassy path, continuing through bracken, in the direction of a distant communication mast. Go with the path as it winds right round a hill and then left round another. Just before the mast, take the path climbing right up yet another ridge. Go on the clear path along the ridge and, where it divides, take the right branch, leading to the top of a hillock. From here you can view the lovely sandy bay of Port Righ. Descend the good path to pass through rhododendrons and bracken. Look for the natural arch on your right. Go down a rocky gully to a rickety stile, with a dog gate beside it. Turn left and follow the path to join a road in front of the houses of Port Righ. Turn right and follow the road as it winds inland. Where it turns sharp right, walk ahead on a wide track lined with fine beech and sycamore. Follow it where it bears right to continue to the village hall, once Carradale Mains. Join the B-road, turn right and walk the quarter of a mile to the car park.

Practicals

Type of walk: This walk has something for everyone. It takes in a fine hill, passes through estate woodland, visits a centre where you can study the cultural background of Carradale and enables you to enjoy the stunning panorama of Arran. It then visits two fine sandy bays, with a delectable headland in between.

Distance: 6 miles/9.6km
Time: 3 hours
Map: OS Explorer 356

5a

Isle of Gigha—Creag Bhan

Park in the second lay-by, grid ref. 654505, beyond (north) Druimyeon farm, north of Ardminish.

The isle of Gigha lies three miles off the Kintyre mainland, opposite the village of Tayinloan from where Caledonian MacBrayne run a regular roll on—roll off ferry. The journey to the unspoilt island takes 20 minutes. Gigha is seven miles long by one and a half wide and a single track road runs from north to south. The shoreline is made up of black rocky inlets, little bays and gorgeous white sandy beaches. A hill ridge forms the centre of the island and culminates in **Creag Bhan,** the highest point at 100m.

On **17 March 2002**, the 110 inhabitants bought the island from the Holt family for £4 million pounds. They received £3 million pounds from Trusts and other Funds and, at the time of writing, they are busy fund raising and asking for pledges of help to raise the remaining £1 million.

1. From the parking area walk back to the farm and turn right, over the cattle grid, onto a metalled track. Climb steadily and follow the way as it swings right. It then bears left, moving out into the rolling countryside passing first below Dunan-an-t Seasgain and then the slopes of Creag Bhan.

Walk 5a

2. Well before the cottage, Ardailly, look for the grassy trod climbing steadily,

24

Merlin

right, towards an inconspicuous small covered reservoir. Pass to the right of this and go on up the generally distinct path through gorse and huge outcrops of granite. Gradually the boulders become larger and fragrant clumps of heather thrive between them. The path now weaves around and between the boulders and there is some easy scrambling to do. Soon you can spot the trig point on the little summit and this keeps you heading in the right direction. When you come upon a difficult boulder to surmount, look where other walkers have found an easier route. Very soon you reach the delectable top, with its stunning view across to the mainland and over the whole length of the island. To the south you might spot the cliffs and mountains of Donegal and, out to sea, Islay and the dramatic hills of Jura. Look north to Knapdale and Kintyre and behind them, east, the peaks of Arran. As you pause here you might also spot a merlin following every twist and turn of its quarry.

Gorse

3. Return by the same route.

Practicals

Type of walk: A short pleasing stroll along a quiet lane, with an exciting quick climb to the top of a rugged little hill.

Distance:	1 ½ miles/2.5km
Time:	1 hour
Map:	OS Explorer 357

5b

Isle of Gigha—Kilchattan and Achamore Gardens

Park beside the Community Hall, grid ref. 645480. To reach this, follow the ferry track to the road that runs throughout the island. Here turn left and, after just over half a mile, turn right.

Ruined **Kilchattan church** (St Cathan's) stands higher up the lane from the Community Hall. It has one fine window still intact. The floor of the building is covered with grave slabs and there are more in the churchyard. Look for the slab in an enclosure, showing a warrior with his sword beside him. The figure is believed to be Malcolm, first MacNeill laird of Gigha, who died in 1493.

In 1944 the island was bought by **Sir James Horlick** who wished to pursue his passion for growing rhododendrons and exotic shrubs. His house, Achamore, already had a parkland of mature trees laid out by previous owners. He added natural windbreaks to these trees, which would protect the tender plants he wished to grow from winter

St Cathan's Church, Gigha

gales and salt spray. After Sir James died he left his plant collection to the National Trust for Scotland. The new owners of the island, the Holt family, together with the Trust pleasingly maintained the gardens and continued to open them to the public. Now that the islanders have bought Gigha, including the gardens (at the time of writing), it is hoped that this partnership between the Trust and the islanders will happily continue.

Walk 5b

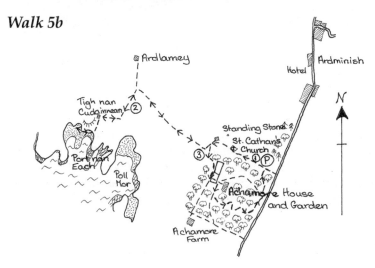

1. Turn right and walk up the lane, with the fine trees of Achamore Gardens to your left. Continue on to visit, on the right, the ruined church of St Cathan. Beyond it, look right to see a fine lichen-encrusted standing stone. Go on to pass a white house on the right and carry on where the way bears left to pass through a gate and over a cattle grid onto a track. Stroll on for half a mile through quiet pastures and, where the track turns right, well before Ardlamey farm, turn left onto another farm track. Here in winter and early spring you might spot a flock of twittering twites descending to the pastures to seek thistle seeds.

2. Press on and go with the grassy way, which bears right to Tigh nan Cudainnean, a cottage with a delightful garden. Just before the dwelling turn left to go through two gates and follow a grassy path down to the rocky shore. Then bear right over the outcrops to come to a stunning sandy bay. Here you will want to idle.

3. Return by the same route until just beyond the cattle grid and the gate close to the white house. A few steps on turn right and walk across the pasture to a wicket gate in the wall of Achamore Gardens. Bear left to another gate and beyond,

Peacocks

begin your delightful stroll through the lovely grounds—a gardener's paradise. Dawdle along the winding walks and through the open glades where, from very early in the year, blossoms colour the way. Banks of rhododendrons, azaleas, camellias and other delightful shrubs are at their most magnificent between March and June. Leave by the side gate—where there is an honesty box to help with the upkeep—that brings you out opposite the Community Hall.

Herring Gull

Practicals

Type of walk: Very easy, generally level walking

Distance: 2 miles/3.4km
Time: 1 hour
Map: OS Explorer 357

6

Clachan and Dun Skeig, Kintyre

Park in the village of Clachan, grid ref. 765561, between the bus stop and the entrance gates to the church, facing the wall alongside the Clachan Burn.

Clachan is believed to be the oldest village in Kintyre. Several pretty cottages and houses stand close to the church of St Colman-Eala, in the ancient parish of Kilcamonell. The present church was built around 1760 on the site of a much older one. Opposite to its main door are a row of magnificent grave slabs, two Early Christian and the others medieval, standing upright and carefully protected by a shelter.

Dun Skeig is a magnificent Iron Age site. The fort encompasses almost the whole hilltop. It has a single wall from which many stones have been robbed. It is described as a vitrified fort in that the stones used to build it were subjected to great heat that caused them to melt. What is not certain is whether this was done on purpose as part of the method of construction or, whether it was accidental. Several families would have lived in the fort and around

Dun Skeig

it would have been ramparts and ditches. Within the wall of the fort are two duns; duns were smaller structures and would have been occupied by one or two families. The dun to the north-east has a well-defined entrance. There is also a cairn and a trig point on the summit. The view from the top is superb.

Walk 6

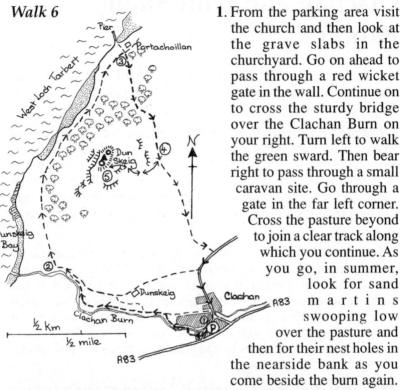

1. From the parking area visit the church and then look at the grave slabs in the churchyard. Go on ahead to pass through a red wicket gate in the wall. Continue on to cross the sturdy bridge over the Clachan Burn on your right. Turn left to walk the green sward. Then bear right to pass through a small caravan site. Go through a gate in the far left corner. Cross the pasture beyond to join a clear track along which you continue. As you go, in summer, look for sand martins swooping low over the pasture and then for their nest holes in the nearside bank as you come beside the burn again. Stride on to join a superb track, coming in on your right, its base composed of small pieces of stone forming a smooth cobbled way.

2. Soon the burn bears away left and heads for Dunskeig Bay on West Loch Tarbert. Continue on to the next gate and pause to enjoy the view of Gigha and Islay across the sparkling sea. You might spot the Islay ferry approaching Kennacraig. The easy-to-walk track continues delightfully on. Look for curlews and hoodie crows. At the next gate the path deteriorates for a short distance and you should wind left round the gatepost through the wicket gate and go on along the very wet way. After a few metres it becomes dry and

30

the cobbling emerges once more. Listen for sedge warblers in the reeds as you stroll on—you could almost dance.

3. The track ends at Portachoillan, where there is a small jetty. Once a ferry plied across the sea loch to a similar pier on the opposite shore. Turn right, off the good track and begin to climb a hedged way. Very soon the track becomes cobbled. Go on up to pass to the left of a cottage. Here the track disappears but carry on along a faint grassy way towards a wood. The little path soon becomes a stream bed, but continue on to arrive at a gate into glorious deciduous woodland. After a short muddy climb a pleasing path carries you on up, with a wall to your left and trees stretching away to the right. Gradually the trees begin to thin and you find you are, unexpectedly, walking a wide way strongly walled on both sides. This is known as the 'ferry road'. In high summer the gap between the walls is almost completely choked with bracken and only a narrow path can be followed. Soon the hedge on the left ends and you can see over the rolling pastures sloping down to the loch.

4. As you near the brow of the hilly track and, just beyond the last clump of trees, the little path comes to an old iron gate in the right hand wall. Climb this onto open rough pasture and walk ahead, soon to pick up a path that bears right . Follow this as it curves left, steadily ascending the lower slopes of Dun Skeig. As soon as you can see the great pile of stones on the summit, head towards it, keeping to the right side of a knoll. After descending a narrow gully, go on up through bracken towards the top. At the Y-junction of paths, take the right branch to come to the entrance into the

Sand Martin

north-east dun. The left branch, easier to climb, brings you to a second dun, a cairn and a trig point.

5. After you have enjoyed the stunning view and the atmospheric ancient remains, leave by the same route to return to the track beyond the gate. Turn right and stride the now pleasing wide way, free of bracken and a joy to walk. In summer it is a glorious floral highway, which descends gently for nearly three-quarters of a mile. It then bears left to join the road. Turn right to go on descending to the parking area at Clachan.

Curlew

Practicals

Type of walk: A fine walk along good tracks for much of the way, at first over pastures and then close to the sea. It then turns inland and climbs steadily to the foot of the easy-to-ascend Dun Skeig.

Distance: 3 ½ miles/5.5km
Time: 2–3 hours
Map: OS Explorer 357

7

Skipness—
Skipness River, moorland slopes of Cnoc Moine Raibeirt, Skipness Point, Chapel and Castle, Kintyre

Park in the visitors' car park, grid ref. 904579, at the end of the B8001. It is situated in a delightful forest clearing opposite and, just beyond, the ornate gates for Skipness Castle.

The iron-age fort of **Dunan Breac** stands on a steep-sided knoll deep in the forest—an easily defended site above the Skipness River. From the tiny grassy summit, there are fine views over the trees to Kilbrannan Sound and the Isle of Arran.

Kilbrannan (St Brendan) Chapel was built between the late 13th and the early 14th century, replacing an earlier one that was once part of Skipness Castle. It lies close to the shore of Skipness Bay and 300m south east of the castle. It is well preserved and has some fine medieval gravestones.

The strategically placed 13th century **Skipness Castle,** overlooks Kilbrannan Sound. It was most likely built by Dugald the son of Sween. Later the castle, perhaps under the guiding hand of Edward

Skipness Castle

I of England, was enlarged and fortified by the MacDonalds of Islay and Kintyre. It then passed to one of the Earls of Argyll and remained in Campbell hands until the mid 1800s.

Walk 7

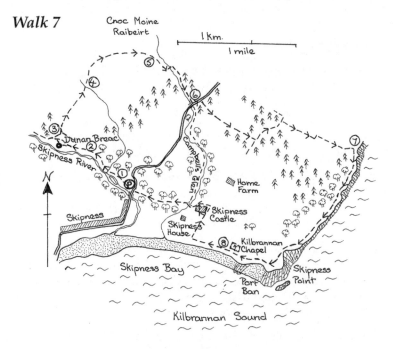

1. Leave the parking area by the signed footpath, a grassy way that leads into glorious deciduous woodland. Where the path comes close to the side of the Skipness River follow the track, right, and stroll on. Cross a tributary burn, ignore a bridge over the river, and continue to a Y-junction of paths. Take the right branch and climb steadily along a path waymarked by a green post. After a few steps bear left, ignoring the narrower path that goes straight ahead. Ascend through oaks, alder and sycamore, with the occasional post to reassure you that you are on the right path. Stroll, with care, along a narrow terraced path, high above the burn, where children and dogs should be under firm control. Pause at a safe spot to look over the magnificent glen, one great mass of deciduous trees through which hurries the turbulent burn.

2. Follow the path as it begins to descend and is railed. To the right, tree-covered slopes rear steeply upwards. Go on up and down

34

several small flights of steps to come to the foot of a ladder of steps to climb a huge rock face. Go on along the continuing path, as it moves away from the burn, to reach a post signed, 'Dun'. Climb a short steep path, as directed, onto the little summit. Take heed of the warning about keeping clear of a sheer edge, where a landslide has occurred. Descend from the dun by an easy slope, to the right of the warning sign, to join the ongoing waymarked path. This soon turns sharp right up a forest ride to a signpost.

3. Turn left in the direction of 'Campbell's Glen via Hill'. Go on along the track to a gate onto moorland and the lower slopes of Cnoc Moine Raibeirt, where you might spot roe deer. Walk ahead on a narrow boggy path towards a clear waymark. Pause by the post to enjoy the view, right, to see the hills about the Cock of Arran and, perhaps, the ferry crossing from Lochranza to Claonaig. Look back to see the Kintyre peninsula, stretching away into the distance. Divert round any small pools and go on towards a post to the right of an obvious willow. As you near this bush follow the narrow path, uphill, beside a hurrying burn, and continue on the path as it winds beyond the willow to an easy place to step across the tumbling water.

Mergansers

4. Walk on and stand beside the marker post. From here look along the same contour to pick out the next two marker posts. Then walk a widish way, where the grass has been mown. This brings you to a continuing stone and turf dyke, where you should keep to its right. Ahead you can see two more dykes heading downhill and, beyond, a scattering of trees lining the next burn. There is no clear path but walk towards the burn over the rough ground, descending towards an arrowed fence corner.

5. Continue down beside the fence until you reach a waymarked gate through it. Beyond, step across the burn and a few paces on, turn

right to walk to a waymarked stile into conifers. Descend the pretty path, close to the stream on your right. Soon the way leaves the trees and passes through long grass to come to a footbridge of conifer poles across a tributary. Beyond, join a forest road, by a signpost.

6. Turn left in the direction of the 'coastal walk'. In a 100m, go right along a well made track, where you pass through three gates to arrive at another signpost. Here turn left, taking the 'coastal path'. Go through the next gate and then walk right through fields, with a fine view ahead. On reaching two gates, take the waymarked one on the right. Walk on and take a gate in the wall on the left to continue on the stiled way towards the shore, now with the wall to your right.

7. Near the shore climb the ladderstile on your right and follow a path through rocky outcrops and lush vegetation. If it has rained heavily overnight you may have to make a few diversions to avoid several wet stretches. Look for rafts of mergansers floating on the waves just off shore. Eventually the way becomes clearer as you continue. Pass through an awkward waymarked hurdle and stroll across a pasture. Soon a good track emerges and winds round delightful Skipness Point, where there is a splendid sandy bay. A very good track leads you close to the ruined chapel.

8. After visiting the chapel return to the waymarked track and follow it as it bears right to visit the castle, which you will want to explore. Leave by the gate through the wall on the north side and turn left. Cross the bridge over the burn and stroll on to the end of the castle road to pass through the large gates. Turn right to return to the car park, which is on the left.

Practicals

Type of walk: A glorious walk that takes you by a river, through woodland to a dun, over moorland, along the seashore and returns you past an ancient chapel and castle.

Distance: 4 miles/6.5km
Time: 3 hours
Map: OS Explorer 357

8

Torinturk, Knapdale

Park in the Forestry Commission's car park, Torinturk, on the B8024, at grid ref. 808641. It lies 400m up a rising track behind the village of the same name.

Diarmid's grave, a bronze age cairn, is reached first on the walk. It is named after a Celtic hero, one of Finn MacCoul's warriors. It is marked by a triangular upright stone and dates from between 2500 and 600 BC. Just beyond the grave is a larger cairn, with several stones visible on top of a mound. This is believed to have been erected by Neolithic farming communities who settled in Kintyre between 4000 and 2000 BC. Bones were placed in the central chamber along with stone tools and food as part of an elaborate burial ritual.

Dairmid's Grave

Dun a' Choin Dubh (Dun of the Black Dog) is reached at the highest point on the walk. This fortified home was built and lived in sometime between the 6th and 11th century AD. Local legend has it that the tunnel below the fort was guarded by a black wolf bitch, which has given its name to the Dun.

Walk 8

1. Read the information panel and then walk south-west along a pleasing terraced track, with conifers stretching steeply upwards to the right. To the left, over younger conifers, you can see West Loch Tarbert, with Kennacraig, the ferry port for Islay, across the water. The pretty pink flower, centaury, grows along the grassy middle of the track. At the waymark (green post with a blue band) turn right and begin to climb a grassy ride, passing through sitka spruce, which lie well back from the track. Continue on to a clearing in the forest and take a short path, half left, to view the burial cairns.

2. Then return to the waymarked main path and go on gently ascending for 200m. At the top of the slope the path levels out. Continue on the wide way as it descends and then at the information board, turn left and begin the steep climb to a ladder stile. Pause on the top step for another fine view, through the tree tops, of Kennacraig, where you might spot the ferry docking. Beyond the stile, climb the steep ramparts of the fort. Once on the top, walk left, to see the tunnel beneath the fort. Enjoy the stunning views from the summit. Look across Loch Tarbert and over the Kintyre peninsula to the hills

Centaury

38

of Arran. Wander, with care, around the wonderful site and appreciate how well it could be defended in times of trouble.

3. Descend the same way to rejoin the main track once more and turn left. At the next T-junction, turn right and go on to the next T-junction and the parking site.

Crossbills

Practicals

Type of walk: Good tracks and paths take you to ancient monuments and outstanding viewpoints. Steep climb to the dun—but take your time because it is well worth the effort..

Distance: 1 mile/1.5km
Time: 1 hour
Map: OS Explorer 357

9

West Loch Tarbert to Tarbert Castle, Kintyre

Park at Corranbuie, grid ref. 843659, on the east side of the A83, at the start of the track that takes you to the castle. If this is full return for ½ mile, north, along the A-road to a lay-by opposite the entrance to West Loch Tarbert Holiday Park

Tarbert Castle was believed to have been built, in the 13th century, by Alexander II or Alexander III. Between 1325 and 1329 the castle was strengthened and extended by Robert I (Robert the Bruce). At that time Bruce decided to confront the chiefs of the Western Isles who were acting as allies of England. He set off across the isthmus of Tarbert to avoid the long and often dangerous sail around Kintyre. To cross the isthmus he had a track of logs put down on the mile-wide neck of land. Over this 'railway' his galleys were dragged, with sails set to take advantage of the wind. He realised the importance of the isthmus and the need to defend it and in 1325 he started on the repair and enlargement of the existing castle, which stood, and still does, on a hill above the village of Tarbert.

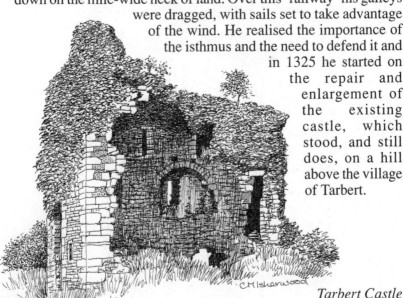

Tarbert Castle

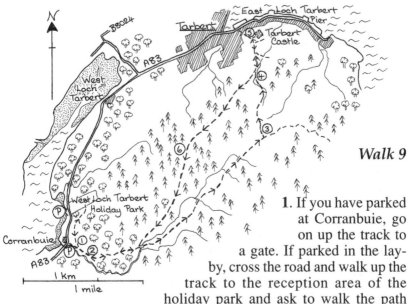

Walk 9

1. If you have parked at Corranbuie, go on up the track to a gate. If parked in the lay-by, cross the road and walk up the track to the reception area of the holiday park and ask to walk the path through the woodland. This is a splendid route put in by the owner and leaves the site opposite the reception chalet. The way takes you, right, through ancient deciduous woodland and after meandering pleasingly through the trees brings you to the gate mentioned above.

2. After passing a forest enterprise board welcoming walkers, go through the gate and walk ahead climbing steadily. In summer the verges are colourful with wild flowers and over these flit many common blue butterflies. To the left of the trail, outcrops of schist support huge banks of heather. After half a mile you reach your first waymarker, with a white footprint. Ignore the left turn and go on ahead along the easy-to-walk track as it passes through open moorland, with many outcrops, cushions of heather and a scattering of deciduous trees. The way continues into coniferous woodland but here the trees lie well back from the route, maintaining the feeling of a lovely open, airy walk. Here you might spot siskins, tree pipits and redpolls, flitting across the track. Once you reach the top of the ridge you can glimpse Loch Fyne and the Cowal peninsula. Follow the track as it begins to descend and comes to a waymarked left turn (blue footprint), which you take.

3. Go down a little, then the path climbs steadily round a bluff. The

41

way becomes grassy as it begins its long descent, and you can see the village of Tarbert below, with East Loch Tarbert beyond. Cross two footbridges, where in summer bog asphodel grows in profusion.

4. At the T-junction turn right and, remaining on the main track, scramble down a steepish railed way. At the next T-junction turn left (now on the red trail). Go on to cross two long stretches of duck-boarding to come to a forest information board. Here turn right to climb two flights of wooden steps to reach the precincts and the ivy and moss-clad ruins of the castle, overlooking Tarbert.

5. Enjoy this pleasant spot, set high above an extensive open space, with outcrops and scattered shrubs. Then return the same way— descending the two sets of steps and turning left. Continue over the duckboarding, turn right and scramble up the railed way to come to the waymarked junction. Here ignore the track on the left, walked earlier, and go ahead along the white footprint way. This leads to a footbridge and good views over Tarbert. Stroll on the wide grassy waymarked track climbing through an open area to reach the top of the ridge.

6. Carry on where conifers come closer to the path, which descends for a long, long way, always grassy and easy on your feet. Eventually you reach the outward main track, where you turn right. Stroll on downhill to the gate at the entrance to the forest trail. Go ahead if parked at Corranbuie, or take the lovely track, right, through the deciduous woodland to the holiday park, where you turn left to descend to the lay-by.

Practicals

Type of walk: This walk is part of several constructed as part of a Millennium Forest for Scotland Project, with financial support from the Millennium Commission and the lottery. It is a walk to a picturesque ruined castle that all the family will enjoy. There are many stunning views along the way.

Distance: 6 ½ miles/10.6km
Time: 3 ½ hours
Map: OS Explorer 357.
   Useful Forestry Commission leaflet 'Tarbert and Skipness'.

10

St Columba's Cave and Chapel,
Steallair Dubh (an ancient track) and Ellary, Knapdale

There are several possible parking places, close to the sign for Columba's Cave, grid ref. 751759, at Chapel Bay. To reach this, take the B8024 to Achahoish. Here turn west along a narrow road that soon comes close to the shore of Loch Caolisport.

Columba's Cave at Cove is believed to be where the saint carried on his ministry while visiting his kinsman King Conal of Dalriada when he was seeking his consent to set up a monastery on the Isle of Iona. A narrow path through lush vegetation leads from the shoreside road to a ruinous 13th century chapel. Beyond, the path continues to a huge cliff, where the rock face is stratified and folded and there are two caves. The smaller, on the left, might have been used as a dormitory. The much larger one is extensive and contains a simple stone altar with, above, an equally simple cross. At the back of the cave stone steps lead to a lower level. This is a very peaceful corner of Knapdale.

St Columba's Cave, Ellary

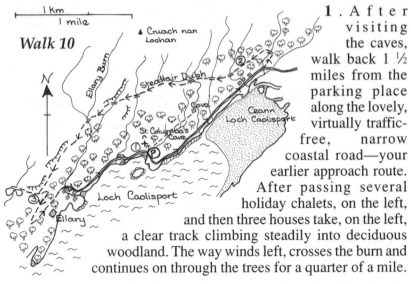

Walk 10

1. After visiting the caves, walk back 1 ½ miles from the parking place along the lovely, virtually traffic-free, narrow coastal road—your earlier approach route. After passing several holiday chalets, on the left, and then three houses take, on the left, a clear track climbing steadily into deciduous woodland. The way winds left, crosses the burn and continues on through the trees for a quarter of a mile.

2. The clear way, an ancient track, waymarked with rather elderly posts, emerges from the trees and continues over the lower moorland slopes of Cruach nan Lochan. Ford a small burn and carry on ascending steadily. Pass a magnificent waterfall where the burn descends in lace-like streams through a tangle of bushes, trees and low-growing plants. The undulating way, sometimes boggy but never in any doubt, goes pleasingly on below craggy outcrops and, where in summer, the verges are spangled with flowers. Eventually, after nearly 3 miles/5km from where you emerged from the trees you reach a seat at the junction of the old track and the reinforced zig-zagged way that descends to Ellary.

Long-tailed tit

44

3. Turn left and stroll the easy track down and down. Look through the trees on the right to see Ellary House. Continue to a small gate beside a large metal one and turn left to walk the tarred road that passes through magnificent deciduous woodland to the shore. (This is the end of the road from Achahoish). Walk left along the road, with a lichen-encrusted wall on the sea side and fascinating rock formations beyond. Enjoy your ¾ mile return walk to rejoin your vehicle, where in spring the banks are lined with primroses and the trees alive with long tailed tits.

Redpoll

Practicals

Type of walk: Half of this fine walk is along an old track high above the coastal road—which is walked first and last. The road is narrow, quiet and flower lined in summer.

Distance: 5 ½ miles/9km
Time: 3 hours
Map: OS Explorer 358

45

11

Taynish Peninsula, Knapdale

Park in the Scottish Natural Heritage small car park, grid ref. 737853, at the end of a narrow, rough road, without passing places, 1 ¼ miles south of Tayvallich.

The Taynish Peninsula has, for 6,000 years, supported woodland, bog, grassland and coastal heath. The peninsula has one of the largest remaining natural oak woodlands in Britain and it has been a National Nature Reserve since 1977. Ferns, lichens and mosses flourish in the warm, wet, west coastal weather. In spring the woodland floor is carpeted with bluebells and primroses. In summer look for common agrimony, hemp agrimony, honeysuckle, yellow flags and foxgloves. The track through the reserve is a haven for speckled wood butterflies, common darter dragonflies and large red damselflies.

Ruined Mill, Taynish

Walk 11

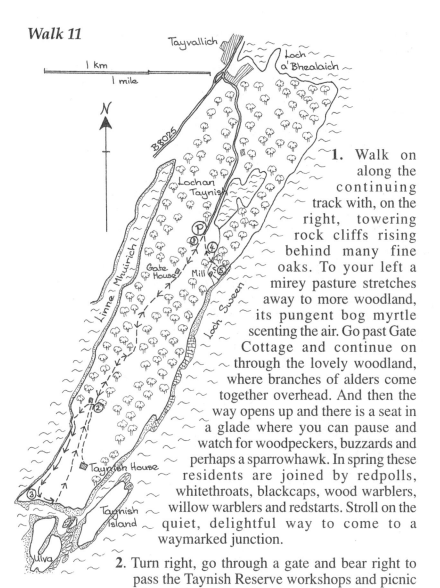

1 km
1 mile

Tayvallich

Loch a'Bhealaich

B8025

Lochan Taynish

Linne Mhuirich

Gate House

Mill

Loch Sween

Taynish House

Taynish Island

Ulva

1. Walk on along the continuing track with, on the right, towering rock cliffs rising behind many fine oaks. To your left a mirey pasture stretches away to more woodland, its pungent bog myrtle scenting the air. Go past Gate Cottage and continue on through the lovely woodland, where branches of alders come together overhead. And then the way opens up and there is a seat in a glade where you can pause and watch for woodpeckers, buzzards and perhaps a sparrowhawk. In spring these residents are joined by redpolls, whitethroats, blackcaps, wood warblers, willow warblers and redstarts. Stroll on the quiet, delightful way to come to a waymarked junction.

2. Turn right, go through a gate and bear right to pass the Taynish Reserve workshops and picnic tables. Then go on along a grassy track to pass through a gate onto duckboarding. Ahead are fine views of the blue waters of Linne Mhuirich—a 'finger' of Loch Sween. Walk ahead to the shoreline. Turn left and find the driest way to edge the wave-licked turf, in June spangled with thrift. Look for oystercatchers, curlews, rock pipits, herring gulls and herons.

3. Wind round a small promontory where, in summer, grow skullcap and silverweed brightening the vegetation. Pause here to look across the water to the Ulva Islands and Taynish Island. Keep a watchful eye for otters along the shore and roe deer on the edge of woodland. Continue to a lichen-covered drystone wall that runs out to sea with, on either side, a flat area for beaching a boat. Go through the gap in the wall and then turn inland along a clear path through yellow flags. Pass through a gate and stroll on along a good track into willow woodland. The pleasing way brings you back to the waymarked Y-junction. Go ahead to return along the track to the parking area. Here, turn right, following the sign for Taynish Mill. The well made track passes through willow and there is another seat for convenient birdwatching.

4. Go on to pass a pretty pool, the mill pond, which received its water from Lochan Taynish, beyond. On the opposite side of the track you can see the mill leat cut through the willows. Follow the path as it zig-zags steadily downhill (this is to help wheelchair users enjoy this lovely corner). As you descend you have a fine view of the old mill, which is being steadily refurbished. Beyond the mill is a clearing with more picnic tables. Pause here and look back to the left side of the mill, where the water from the leat tumbles down a slope—once it would have powered the mill wheel.

Speckled Wood

5. Stride on along the path which brings you to the edge of Loch Sween. There is another seat here to enjoy the view across the sea loch. Watch for seals on the rocks and for gannets diving after fish. Return by the same route.

Practicals

Type of walk: On this delightful walk through what is often called 'the hidden peninsula' there is always something to see. It is a level walk on good tracks, except along the shoreline where, if you take your time, you can pick your way dryshod.

Distance: 4 ½ miles/7.4km
Time: 2 hours
Map: OS Explorer 358

Crinan Canal

Park in the free car park, nearest to the swing bridge and the sea loch, at Ardrishaig, grid ref. 853854.

The 9-mile long **Crinan canal** allows boats to journey across the narrow isthmus, at the north end of the Kintyre peninsula, between the sea lochs of Crinan and Gilp. It was designed by John Rennie and construction started in the 1790s. It was finished in 1809 and in 1817 it was improved by Thomas Telford. Once in use, boats were able to avoid the long and dangerous passage around the Mull of Kintyre. Eight locks, between Ardrishaig and Cairnbaan, raise the boats 20m above sea-level. Seven lower them back down between Dunardry and Crinan. For much of its length the canal follows a raised beach, which marks the line of a post-ice age sea shore.

Dunardry Bridge, Crinan Canal

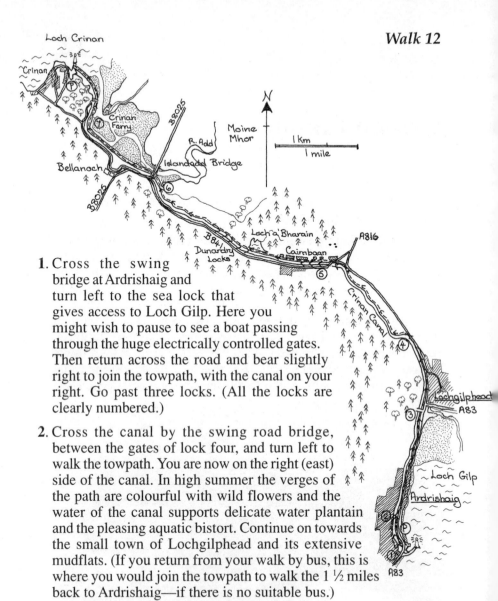

Loch Crinan

Crinan

Crinan
Ferry

B8025

R. Add

Moine
Mhor

Islandadd Bridge

Bellanoch

B8025

1 Km
1 mile

N

Loch a' Bharain

Dunardry
Locks

Cairnbaan

A816

Crinan Canal

Lochgilphead

A83

Loch Gilp

Ardrishaig

A83

1. Cross the swing bridge at Ardrishaig and turn left to the sea lock that gives access to Loch Gilp. Here you might wish to pause to see a boat passing through the huge electrically controlled gates. Then return across the road and bear slightly right to join the towpath, with the canal on your right. Go past three locks. (All the locks are clearly numbered.)

2. Cross the canal by the swing road bridge, between the gates of lock four, and turn left to walk the towpath. You are now on the right (east) side of the canal. In high summer the verges of the path are colourful with wild flowers and the water of the canal supports delicate water plantain and the pleasing aquatic bistort. Continue on towards the small town of Lochgilphead and its extensive mudflats. (If you return from your walk by bus, this is where you would join the towpath to walk the 1 ½ miles back to Ardrishaig—if there is no suitable bus.)

3. Stroll on to Oakfield Bridge or Miller's Bridge, named after a William Miller who earned, in 1854, £16 a year for maintaining it. Here an interesting plaque explains that, in earlier times, sediment washed down by streams into the canal resulted in it having to be dredged. The mud and silt were thrown onto the canal bank and when plants colonised the soil they were cut and lime added. These unusual conditions have resulted in the glorious array of flowers, common-spotted orchids being a speciality—they range from white through pink to dark purple. Do not cross the bridge but stroll on past anglers fishing for sea trout.

4. Then the canal moves away from the parallel road and the path is quieter. High up, on the opposite bank, tall conifers provide a fine backdrop for a great variety of deciduous trees, which descend steeply to the edge of the water. Look carefully, in midsummer, along this stretch, for a myriad of butterfly orchids growing along the verges of the path. And then you arrive at Cairnbaan, where there is a hotel. This was once a drovers' inn in the days when hundreds of cattle from the islands and Highlands would be driven slowly to market. There is one lock before the swing bridge—which you do NOT cross. You are now at the highest point of the canal.

Butterfly Orchids

5. Continue on, still on the right side of the cut, along a vehicle track, to pass several cottages. Soon the way reverts to a path. Walk on to lock nine, with Loch a'Bharain to the right. Opposite is the Dunardry Burn feeder stream carrying water from Daill loch. Lock nine is the start of the Dunardry locks. By lock eleven is Dunardry rolling bridge, which was installed in 1900. It runs on rails and is wound back by hand. Continue on to pass through a gate. Away to your right stretches the great moss of Moine Mhor. The towpath now takes you into the Scottish Natural Heritage Moine Mhor National Nature reserve.

6. Look ahead and right as you go to see the fine Islandadd Bridge, which dates from 1851—a graceful five span cast-iron structure below which idles the Add River. Look back from here to see Dunadd Hill and fort (walk 13b). Look also for oyster catchers, curlews, redshanks and mergansers on the sands or in the shallows. The towpath continues with the estuary close beside it to the right and, with Bellanoch basin, used as a marina, to the left. The basin is edged by some fine houses and high up on a green hill stands a white chapel.

7. Soon the way narrows and the road swings away over the hill to Crinan. Pass another swing bridge and a bridge keeper's cottage. Opposite (across the Add) is Crinan Ferry where a boat used to cross the estuary. Lush vegetation covers the huge rock face on the opposite bank. Follow the towpath as the canal winds round the craggy headland and continue into Crinan, with its massive sea lock, hotel and cafe. It is a busy place with yachts coming and going and a fine place to sit and watch all the activity.

Practicals

Type of walk: An amazing lush interlude between two bits of sea!

Distance: 9 miles/15km of level walking—and 9 miles back unless you can arrange for someone to pick you up or, walk with friends and use two cars. If you decide to return by bus, don't forget to sort out times before you start. For details telephone (01546 602344) the Lochgilphead tourist information office (open April to October) or use the public transport helpline, 01546 604695 (Argyll and Bute Council).

Time: 4–5 hours one way

Map: OS Explorer 358

Kilmartin Glen

Park at Lady Glassary Wood, grid ref. 829975. The parking area lies just off the A816, a mile south of the village of Kilmartin.

Kilmartin Glen reveals traces of human habitation dating back over 5,000 years. Today the dale is known as the 'linear cemetery' because of its row of chambered cairns that stretch along the lovely valley floor. From around 3000 BC the dead were buried in a stone box-shaped grave, part of a vast tomb. When the grave became full another was built. When the tomb was full, the entrance was sealed and a huge cairn of stones was placed on top. This continued over many 100s of years.

Carnasserie Castle, high on a ridge above the Kilmartin valley, is a 16th century combined tower and hall-house. It was built by John Carswell, Rector of Kilmartin and who, from 1567, was Bishop of Argyll and the Isles. Later it was held by the Campbells of Achnabreck. It 1685 it was captured and partly blown up during the ninth Earl of Argyll's rebellion against James VII. It is an exciting castle to visit, one which youngsters will enjoy. It is open at all reasonable times.

Burial Cairn, Kilmartin

1. Turn left out of the parking area and walk along the narrow road, with the Nether Largie standing stones across the pasture to your right. Continue on, with the alder-shaded Kilmartin burn to your right, and then take the first right turn to cross the burn and walk on.

2. A short distance along, look for the arrow directing you, left, to the Ri Cruin cairn. It is the most southerly of Kilmartin's 2km linear cemetery and is believed to date from around 2000 BC. It is approached by a pleasing track between a wall and a fence. The site is idyllic, the cairn standing in a grassy area surrounded by sycamore, beech, lime, ash and elm. Return to the road and continue on. Just before the road sign for the village of Slockavullin, turn right to walk another quiet lane, now with the standing stones away to the right.

3. Stroll on to, on the left, the Temple Wood Circles. This site is believed to have been in use for over 2,000 years from about 3500 BC. The dramatic southern circle of stones was probably placed in position about 2000 BC. The northern circle replaced a timbered henge, but was never completed. It was constructed before 3000 BC. Look for the sockets for the timber posts. Walk on from the circles to turn left (not sharp left) into the old coach road. Pass, on your left, the 19th century primary school and walk on to a stile on the right.

Carnasserie Castle

A816

Upper Largie

N

Gravel Pit

Kilmartin Museum
Church
Glebe Cairn

North Cairn
Nether Largie
Mid Cairn

School

Temple Wood Circles
Nether Largie South Cairn

Walk 13a

Slockavullin

Standing Stones

Lady Glassary Wood

½ km

½ mile

Ri Cruin Cairn

B8025

A816

4. A fenced path leads to Nether Largie mid cairn. When excavated in 1929 two cists (single stone burial boxes dug into the ground and covered with a capstone) were found, one decorated with carvings of axeheads. Return to the coach road and walk on to Nether Largie north cairn. This has been rebuilt and you can enter from the top by a modern sliding door to see the intriguing inner chamber and a cist cover decorated with carved axeheads and cup marks. The site dates from 2000–1500 BC.

5. Return again to the coach road and stroll on along the delightful lane. Ignore the footbridge on your right and go on to pass through the next gate, continuing on the coach road. After the next gate, cross the burn, where in spring kingcups flower, to join a wide quarry track. Bear left then take the left fork and carry on with the burn to your left, passing through quarry buildings. Stroll round the edge of a fenced gravel pit to take the right branch where the way divides. From here you can see Carnasserie Castle straight ahead through the trees.

6. Follow the track along the left edge of a pasture and go through three gates, with a low wall and fence to your left—still on the old coach road. Where the fence ends the way follows a raised bank with a wide ditch to the left and, beyond the ditch, a walled garden. Go through the gate at the end of the way on to a farm track. Turn right and then almost immediately left through another gate to follow the coach road.

7. Continue through scattered deciduous trees, where in spring you might hear a redstart and, if lucky, a grasshopper warbler, to a gate. Beyond press on along the clear track until it curves left, with the castle ahead and slightly right. At this point, leave the track and cross the pasture to go through a gap in the wall. Turn right and descend to a gate. Beyond, go down through a wood to join the main track to the dramatic ruin, which you reach by climbing steps on your left, and spend time exploring. Return back up the hill to the gap in the wall and continue across the pasture to join the track. Turn left and go on downhill to the gate through the delightful scattered trees. Continue to the gate on to the track and, this time,

Redstart

turn left to pass Upper Largie farm. Follow the track as it winds right and continue on until you reach the garage at the edge of Kilmartin. Head on along the path below the road, protected by a wall, to walk into the village to visit Kilmartin church.

8. It was built in 1836 replacing earlier churches of 1798 and 1601. Inside and in the churchyard look for the extensive fine collection of medieval graveslabs, many with carvings of swords, crosses and armoured figures. Also look for the Kilmartin Cross, with its simple carving of Christ. Leave time to visit the heritage centre and the museum of ancient culture. Then return along the walled path beside the road to the kissing gate just before the garage. Beyond, follow the path across the pasture to a huge mound of boulders, known as Glebe cairn, a burial cairn dating from 2000–1500 BC. Continue on the path to the footbridge in the corner of the field—the one you ignored earlier. Turn left to walk back along the coach road. Pass the primary school and, at the junction, take the second turn on the right. Carry on to the signed track, on the left, to visit Nether Largie south cairn, which you can enter. This has a substantial stone chamber built to receive the bones of the dead over several generations. It is older than the other cairns visited, possibly dating from 3000 BC.

9. Take the fenced path beyond the cairn in the direction of Lady Glassary Wood. Follow the way as it turns right and on to a gate. Beyond make your way over to the standing stones and look for the intriguing carvings. It is believed that, together with the Temple Wood circles, they were part of a lunar observatory. Continue on from the stones to cross the burn to return to the parking area.

Practicals

Type of walk: This is a wonderful level walk, through the quiet picturesque Kilmartin Glen. Enjoy its castle and its many archaeological treasures—a must for everyone's walking holiday.

Distance:	5 miles/8km
Time:	As much time as you can spare—there is so much to see.
Map:	OS Explorer 358

Dunadd fort

Park at the foot of Dunadd Hill, grid ref. 838935

    The early Scottish kingdom of Dalriada (AD 500) was centred on **Kilmartin Glen**. At the heart of this kingdom, and possibly its capital, was Dunadd fort, built on the imposing rocky hill of Dunadd, once a Pictish defensive site.

Dunadd

1. Walk from the parking area to a gate at the foot of the hill. Beyond bear left and begin to climb the rocky way. Follow the path as it gently winds round right, pausing on the way to look over the extensive peaty pasture of Moine Mhor. Away over the great moss you can see the masts on the boats of the Crinan Canal (walk 12). Go on up a delightful rocky defile where, in summer, grow pink stonecrop and sweet-smelling heather.

Walk 13b

2. At the top of defile is a large terrace, with a tumbledown wall, which once protected the king's subjects. To its right side is a circular grid-covered well, dedicated to St Columba. The saint was a kinsman of the first Dalriadan king (Aidan) and, in AD 574, Columba performed his coronation here. Then climb on again through another narrow cleft. At the top bear left to see the carved 'footprint of fealty' in a stone slab and a hollow basin—the anointing stoup—both believed to have been used in the inauguration of the kings. On the same rock you can see the faint

Stonecrop

outline of a boar, which is thought to be of Pictish origin—the Picts sometimes recaptured the fortress! On the slab beyond is a cup and ring mark. Go on up to the large rocky summit, the site of the fort, for a superb view. Look down on the fine meanders of the River Add, snaking across the flat land to the inner reaches of Loch Crinan. Return the same way.

Primroses, Wood Sorrel and Golden Saxifrage

Practicals

Type of walk: This is a short easy climb to a superb viewpoint, where you will want to ponder on all that happened here.

Distance:	½ mile/0.8km
Time:	½ hour
Map:	OS Explorer 358

From Loch Awe to Loch Fyne
A linear walk along the Leacan Muir (Broad High Moor) route.

This 11-mile linear walk requires some careful planning and will need two cars unless you have a kindly friend who will drop you off at Kilneuair and pick you up at Auchindrain. Leave one vehicle in the second lay-by, east of the Rights-of-Way Society sign, Kilneuair, 1 ½ miles east of Ford, grid ref. 889038. The second car should be left in the large lay-by behind the Rights of Way Society sign, Auchindrain, grid ref. 028033.

It is difficult to imagine that this long trackway over wild moorland was once thronged with travellers using what was a **major route across mid-Argyll**. The way is remote, lonely and atmospheric. Round each knoll and at the top of each rise, you expect first to hear, and then to join, a string of ponies carrying charcoal for the furnaces of Loch Fyne. Near the misty high parts and reed-fringed lochs you feel that you might have to move out of the way of a herd of cattle lumbering towards Inveraray and the south. Local people were expected, by law, to keep the old route maintained and in good repair. Today it is still good in most parts and generally easy to walk.

Packhorse bridge, Leacan Muir

Kilneuair Chapel, a picturesque ruin, is visited almost at the start of the walk. Here worshipped the inhabitants of the whole area. Large important markets were held in this quiet corner. Look for the faint 'Devil's Handprint' on the dressed stone block on the left side (as you leave) of the doorway of the ruin. Legend attributes it to the devil's huge unearthly hand that grasped the block as the spectre was chasing a man who boasted that darkness had no power. The man had accepted a challenge to spend the night in the haunted precincts of the chapel and on seeing the grisly hand trying to grab him had fled in terror.

Walk 14

1. Climb the track, below spruce, as directed by the signpost, to reach the chapel in a clearing. Continue on and, at a gate, take a stile over the fence on the left. Cross a recent track and go on climbing gently as the way winds left and then right. Look back to enjoy the views down to the tree-fringed Loch Awe and of the ruins of Fincharn Castle on its promontory. The clear track continues to the foot of a hillock. Here curve left and then right and go on to cross another modern track.

2. Go ahead and at the next gate, take the stile on the left. Descend to a wet hollow and then pass through hillocky humps, the path winding upwards, with a low bank on either side. Follow the sturdy

60

undulating track as it descends to cross a large flat area, surrounded by hills, with extensive areas of bog cotton and bog myrtle on either side. Climb up the other side of the hollow with a glimpse of trees away to the far right. The path then descends again to a ford over the burn that flows from Loch nan Ceard Mor into Loch Gaineanhach—the Sandy loch. (If the ford is deep the best place to cross is on the exposed shingle close to where the burn enters into Sandy loch.)

3. Beyond, ascend the path to cross an easier ford and go on up the steepish way to pass a ruined shieling, a summer shepherd's hut. Follow the path as it turns right, passing a fine waterfall on the left. The way then climbs to a low ridge, followed by a hairpin bend. Go on up into the high heather moorland to pass a loch close beside you to the left and then another to the right, with a narrow shallow burn linking the two—and another easy ford. Then you reach the summit, Sidh Mor, which means 'big fairy hill'.

4. Go on along the high level path to look down on large Loch a' Chaorainn (loch of sheep). Pause here to enjoy the view ahead of the mountains beyond the forests of conifers. Look to the right for your first glimpse of Loch Fyne. Then begin your long descent of the reasonably good track. Pass through a fence and continue towards a ruin, Carron, an old shepherd's hut. Beside it, on the right, is a building restored and beautifully maintained by the Mountain Bothy Association—where if the weather has changed you might wish to eat your packed lunch.

5. Go on down the track and follow it as it winds left, with the infant River Add beyond. Head on towards a sheep fank and then cross the river on a picturesque gated packhorse bridge. Carry on to a ruined house and then continue on the good track, with a turf and stone wall on either side, and conifers over the wall

Bog Myrtle

on the right. After entering the forest the path soon becomes narrow and very rough. Eventually the way widens and is grassy but, alas, too soon it continues as a reinforced forest road. Head on through the extensive conifers, where occasionally you pass through a clear-felled area and there is a spectacular view towards the hills at the head of Loch Fyne. Continue on the metalled way with fields to the right and forest to the left.

6. Beyond the farm at Brenchoillie, cross the Leacainn Water on another delightful packhorse bridge (with a new bridge beside it for vehicles). The track goes straight on to Auchindrain.

*Bog cotton
(or Cotton grass)*

C.M.Isherwood

Practicals

Type of walk: Challenging, exhilarating and long, through lonely high level moorland. The forest section is less exciting. The path is never in any doubt. Not a walk for a misty day.

Distance: 11 miles/18km
Time: 5–6 hours
Map: OS Explorer 358 and 360

Furnace–Auchindrain—
the Leacainn Trail

Park before the post office in the village of Furnace, grid ref. 023001. To reach this, take the second turn off the A83, Inveraray to Lochgilphead/Campbeltown road and then left again, immediately into a small gravelled parking space.

The **six mile circular route**, set up by the Amenity Group of the village, along the banks of the River Leacainn links Furnace, one of the first industrial villages in the Highlands, to the farm township museum at Auchindrain. Beneath the rock climbers' challenge of Dun Leacainn, there is a wealth of industrial relics, ancient farmland, woods and forest. Before the iron smelting furnace was built in 1755 the village was called Inverleacainn, the mouth of the River Leacainn. But more than the name was to change when in 1841 the granite quarry opened and then the gunpowder works. After coal supplanted charcoal much of the depleted, oak,

'Roman' Bridge, Leacainn Water

ash, birch and elm were replaced by plantation species. Many animals and bird live in the forest. Look for woodpeckers, deer, red squirrels and perhaps the elusive pine martin.

The open-air museum of **Auchindrain Township** is passed about half way round on this six mile walk. Several houses and barns, a stable, shed, smiddy and kiln have been pleasingly restored. They have been furnished in the style of various periods to give a fascinating picture of what life was really like, in past centuries, for the Highlander in this lovely glen.

1. From the parking area go on past the post office and general store and then the village hall. Keep right of the war memorial and pass the Furnace Inn. Cross the bridge over the River Leacainn, hurrying on its way to join Loch Fyne. Bear steadily right to come to the ruined iron-ore blast furnace, after which the village takes its name. It was built here by the Duddon Company of Cumbria, who realised the advantage of Argyll's plentiful supply of charcoal, the nearby river's power and the proximity to sea transport. The works closed in 1813 when charcoal gave way to coal and the steam engine. Return along the road to a waymarker, with a white arrow, directing you, right, up a forest track. Where the track swings right, a waymark sends you straight ahead along a pleasing ride through the forest.

2. Carry on to a signpost, pointing left. Go through the trees to come to a huge boulder, Clach a'Mhadaidh, the wolf stone. Walk round it and notice its patterning and then return to the track once more. Press on through the trees. Soon you are able to look, left, across the glen, with the conifers towering above you only on the right. Continue until you reach a series of steps, taking you up to join a higher stretch of the forest track. Follow this for nearly three-quarters of a mile, with the conifers still beside you on the right. Finally the way climbs a steep slope through clearfell and arrives at a bridge.

3. Cross and turn left beyond a low wall. Go over the hill crest and begin to descend. Cross a wall and then, with care, descend a steep slope. Pause to look at the fine waterfall on the burn to your left. Carry on down a narrow spur, using the sturdy steps, to take a path across what is at present an area of clearfell to a forest track. Cross it and, just before the main road, take a path parallel to it, which

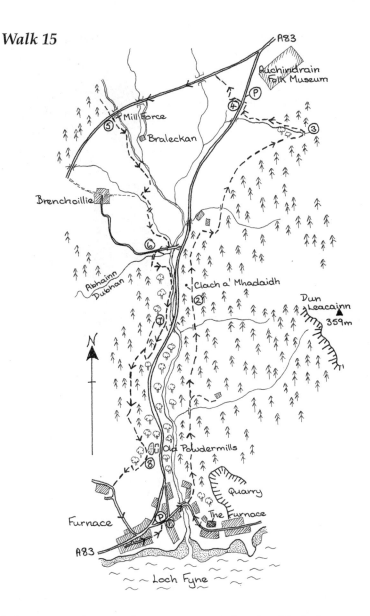

brings you close to the entrance to the Auchindrain township museum, which you may wish to visit.

4. Cross the road with care and take the signposted path opposite. This takes you over rough pasture to the forest road, part of the right of way to Lochaweside (and the end of walk 14). Turn left and follow the way until it crosses a lovely arched bridge, with a new bridge for forestry lorries beside it.

5. Beyond the arched bridge, turn left through a kissing gate and wind downhill. Pause here to look back to see the magnificent waterfall, the Mill Fall. Continue down the bank, high above the River Leacainn, to pass the remains of a corn drying kiln on the left. Carry on through beech and oak. At the foot of the slope, turn right to follow round outside a fenced pasture, turning left at the end. Go through a kissing gate to cross a track. Look for the tributary burn on the right as it flows under a tiny double arched bridge. Go through the gate on the far side of the track, cross the wooden footbridge over the

Great Spotted Woodpecker

hurrying stream, then follow the tributary which joins the Leacainn just before you come to a kissing gate. Beyond, join another track, where you turn right—but first, look left to see another much larger fine double arched bridge over the river. From this point in the walk there is a superb view of Dun Leacainn, towering above its skirts of conifers, through which you walked earlier.

6. After turning right, walk on a short distance to the next waymark, directing you left to a strong modern bridge over the Abhain Dubhan. Follow a good path to a gate and beyond go left on a rather wet way. Follow it as it winds right. Look for the signpost pointing towards a 'Roman' Bridge—not Roman but very old. Go on along the lovely way to notice the Powdermill sluice and then walk the now waterless Powdermill lade, a delectable path, level and banked on either side where, in spring, grow a profusion of wild flowers.

7. Ignore the wide track, on the left, that leads down to the A-road and go ahead along a grassy forest track. This steadily curves right, turning round on itself, to a waymark. This points you sharp left along a slightly rougher narrower track that climbs steadily into more forest. At the signpost look right to see if you can spot several level areas. These were once charcoal burning platforms. Then follow the track as it bears left and begins to descend to pass through a gate. Look left to see a large pool, colonised by reeds and horsetails. On the other side of the water, almost hidden by trees, stand the forlorn remains of several buildings. This is the site of the old gunpowder works, which exploited the same resources as the furnace. The water flowed from the river along the lade you have just walked, into the dam which is now a reed bed. The mill was criticised, under the explosives act of 1875, for siting the 80 ton storage magazine 80 metres from the school. Eight years later the manager died in an explosion causing the closure of the mill.

8. Go on to pass through a gate to walk a wide raised track through a field. Beyond a gate on the right, descend left along the farm's access track to the A-road. Cross and walk right for a few steps to take a quiet road that swings left into a housing estate. At its end continue on a footpath, half left, through a grassy glade to come to the car park beside the post office.

Practicals

Type of walk: A delightful walk that is full of interest throughout. Furnace's Amenity Group should be congratulated.

Distance:	6 miles/9.8km
Time:	3 hours
Map:	OS Explorer 360

16

Craobh Haven, Craignish Peninsula

Park in the large car park at Craobh Haven, grid ref. 795076, a holiday village, approached by a poorly surfaced road that leaves, south-west, off the A816.

As a large force of Vikings neared the **Bay of the Field of Heads** (Bagh Dail nan Ceann) the Celtic occupants of the fortress of Dun Ailne watched their approach. It is easy to image as you stand on the dun the fearsome horde rushing down the slopes, through the gap in the hills, to slay the raiders as they came ashore. On your return along the shore, pause in the bay and look up to see the dun. Then look to the southern arm of the bay to spot a couple of cairns. It is believed that these mark the burial place of those slain in the bloody battle.

Carved stone, Craignish

Corryvrechan, the famous spectacular whirlpool, lies between the islands of Scarba and Jura. During a strong westerly wind and a high tide the whirlpool is likely to be at its most ferocious. It is possible from this walk to see the white water and maybe to hear its roar. The whirlpool is believed to be caused by a tall pillar of rock, about 270m off the Scarba shore, the top of which is about 27m below the surface. The Gulf of Corryvrechan is 280m deep in places. When tides hit the submerged pillar water rushes over it, setting up the continuous whirling of water.

1. Leave the car park to the south of the Lord of the Isles pub. Turn left in front of the village stores and walk up between the modern houses. Pass the 'Giving Tree' bakers and coffee shop, and walk right. Ignore the next left turn and go ahead following the sign for 'Stables'. At the Y-junction take the left fork and again at the next one. Go on towards the fine Lunga House, with its rounded turrets and crow-stepping. Swing round right towards the house and, just before it, take a track off right which then curves left to join a lower one. Walk on, cross a small stream and ignore any minor paths on the left or right. Ignore the access track, on the right, to Lunga Mill, with its skeletal waterwheel still in place, and go ahead to take a gate onto a rough farm track, faintly signed 'Gemmil'.

2. Press on through a copse of birch and oak. Stroll

Walk 16

69

the track as it crosses an open area, with the western slopes of Dun Glas, away to your left. The track ends at the tiny remote cottage of Gemmil. Go on a few yards to a small rocky outcrop, where the indistinct path divides. Ignore the clearer one that passes under larch and descends, right, to the shore and take, instead, a faint path that leads diagonally, across marshy ground, to the far left corner of the pasture. Here, under alders and where the burn turns sharp right, is a shallow ford, which you cross.

3. Go on ahead across the next rough pasture to a large iron gate, with an L set into its bars (L for Lunga). Before this you may have to divert to the right to wind round on a better track to the gate to avoid wet ground. Go through the gate and look back to see Loch Melfort framed by tree-clad hills. Look also for the huge boulder, which stands on the shore, projecting through the intervening trees like a great fang. Go on along the clear path, with cliffs away to your left. It continues below a clump of silver birch and then you can see the Iron-Age fort of Dun Ailne ahead. Follow the path towards it.

4. At the foot of the slopes to the dun take the right of two paths. This lovely way ascends straight up the ridge and comes to the dramatic site. There is little trace of the stonework of the dun but the square platform around the summit seems significant. Look right to see Jura and Scarba and the white water around Corryvrechan—if the tide is right. Leave the top by the far right corner and wind right, and then left, to curve round the foot of the dun. Carry on ahead in the same general direction as before. Go through a gap in a boundary wall and on along the little ridge, with hillocks and sea to the right

and craggy tops to the left. The clear way brings you to what might have been another dun, with fine views down to the coast. Leave again by the far right corner and wind downhill to join a clear path in a gully. The way winds left to a stream over which you step. Take the clear path that goes on upward and over a pasture to a farm gate, incongruously painted pink.

5. After looking to the far right to spot the Paps of Jura, follow the clear path that descends left to a reinforced track. Turn right to pass Barrakan, which once must have been a fine house. Go through the gate, beyond the house, to start your return to Craobh Haven— but first, look left, to a delightful bay with lots of little promontories and tiny islands. Follow a pleasing grassy track, right, which runs below high slopes to the right. The track ends at a stream and just before some sheep pens. A few steps left, look for a little rocky mound to see a carved stone, Leac an Duine, the stone of the just man. Go on across the delectable sward to a gate in the fence under the towering cliffs on your right. Beyond, carry on, enjoying the superb seascape ahead, to pass through the next gate, also in the right corner of the fence. Continue on to the Bay of the Field of Heads from where you can look out to the sprawling mass of the island of Scarba and, beyond, the islands of Luing and Shuna.

6. The next section of the shoreline is much more challenging and, if this is not for you, you may wish to head inland along the wide grassy valley, behind the bay. This will bring you to your outward route, where you should turn left towards the birch trees passed below on your outward route. To continue along the shore be prepared to move into a tangle of birches, with only animal tracks to help you find the easiest way. Keep as near to the shore as possible

Shag

and on reaching a fence, step over where, nearer the shore, there are no barbs. Then walk on to Port Caol. If you wish to escape the shore route here, look for a tractor wheel marked way, over the marsh, which heads inland. This brings you to a better path that winds left to Gemmil—the path you ignored earlier.

7. To head on along the shore, walk towards the immensely high fang-like rock seen before. It is part of a geological dyke running out to sea. Pass through the gap in the wall between the 'fang' and more of the dyke. Pause to look at the marvellous amphitheatre of cliffs that edge the fang. Then move into more birch woodland. Here, as before, there is no path but persevere to come out of the trees close to the cottage at Port Mhic Isaac. Again you can escape inland by walking up the track to come to Lunga House, where you bear left.

8. Stroll on along the shoreline and then steadily descend to a little causeway pier. Wind round the bay, Bagh an Tigh Stoir, first on a good track. Turn off this onto a grass track, on the left, before the good track enters a wood and becomes the access route to a house. Stride on along the continuing rough track. This leads to an open pasture. Keep as close to the shore as possible and, as you approach a fence take a gate, on the far right, hidden by an outcrop. Beyond go on along a narrow path that leads to a wider track. Follow this to a still wider track, where you turn left to walk into Craobh Haven.

Practicals

Type of walk: This is a great walk along a rib of the Craignish peninsula. The outward route is generally clear and easy to walk though after rain the way can be muddy. The return along the shoreline is challenging but there are three escape routes if you prefer a less arduous way.

Distance: 6 miles/9.8km
Time: 4 hours
Map: OS Explorers 358 and 359

17

Loch Avich and Loch Awe

Park at Barnaline car park and picnic site, grid ref. 969139. This lies north of Dalavich on the west side of Loch Awe.

Loch Awe fills a long steep-sided glacial trough. Above, on its west side, forested hills are interspersed with small lochs. The largest is **Loch Avich** out of which drains the River Avich, cascading down its own steep narrow valley on the way to Loch Awe. Half way to the larger loch the river falls in three cascades across open rocks; in spate these are an awesome sight. Below the lowest cascade is a grassy area where Forest Enterprise have placed a picnic table.

Falls of Avich

1. From the parking area, return to the narrow road and turn left. Cross the bridge over the River Avich and follow the road as it continues close beside the hurrying water. Then take the first left, in the direction of Kilmelford, soon to bear left again along a forest track, named 'River Road' and signed with a blue footprint. As you walk the wide easy track look for crossbills about the tops of the conifers and listen for the noise of the hurrying river hidden deep in the forest vegetation. Continue on until you can see the Avich falls, on the left, a few metres off the track.

2. Return to the track and, accompanied by the sound of the surging burn, enjoy the deciduous trees that line both sides of the way, with the conifers of the plantation set well back. Through the trees, you can glimpse Loch Avich and then you continue beside it. All too soon the good track begins to move away from the lovely loch and passes through tall conifers to a gate. This is the end of the 'River Road' and is where you join the narrow road to Kilmelford again. Turn right and climb the short hill.

3. Almost immediately take, on the left, a high-level forest track, overlooking Gleann Meashan, with the Ghlinne burn below; out of sight but not out of sound. Follow this track for two miles. As you progress you pass through clearings among the trees where the grass is as tawny as the deer which inhabit these glades. Along the track you might spot many shiny black droppings of pine martens and you might just, by chance, see one. Continue on and on, ignoring all tracks going off left and right, to cross a tractor bridge and then a concrete bridge, with a pretty fall upstream. The track descends and is edged with deciduous trees, delicate in spring and riotously coloured in autumn. The way carries on through more conifers, where the calls of robins, tits, siskins, goldcrests and coal tits fill the air.

Walk 17

Abhainn Fionain
Waterfa
Gleann Meashan
Allt Ghlinne
Loch Avich
R. Avich
Avich Falls
Kames Bay
Barnaline Lodge
Dalavich
1 Km
1 mile

74

4. Where the track begins to climb slightly, watch out for the red trail (red footprint), going off left. This is a narrower way, soon to become a grassy path, winding through heather. It steadily descends, passing below glorious oak and beech, with a noisy stream to the right. Carry on along the path to cross the Abhainn Fionain on a sturdy bridge. Below, the burn tumbles in a superb fall. Climb the slope beyond, and carry on to a picnic table. Pause here to enjoy the extensive view into the fine steep-sided glen of deciduous trees.

5. Beyond the table, the way swings right and passes through a wide open area, high above a deep gorge, with a tributary stream hidden from sight. Then the path winds gently down to a ford across the stream. Climb the slope to join a reinforced track—the old road into Inverinan Glen. Continue ahead (right) along it, passing between sweet-smelling conifers, with Loch Awe eventually coming into sight. Finally the trees are left behind and the good track descends to Inverinan.

6. Turn right to walk the road for nearly a mile. Turn left onto the Druimdarroch Road, a forest road with a cycle track sign. Follow it as it swings right and continues parallel with Loch Awe, of which you can see glimpses through the trees. Cross the Barr nam Breacadh peninsula, when all sight of the long loch is lost. Continue along Kames Bay, where you are by the water again. Then press on along the track as it moves inland, with fine backward views of the loch from here, to join the road again. Turn left, cross the bridge over the River Avich and carry on to the car park.

Practicals

Type of walk: This is a long walk nearly all on forest roads with a reasonable surface and gradient. It is just the walk for when you wish to escape the wind that sometimes afflicts Argyll.

Distance: 9 ½ miles/15.4km
Time: 4–5 hours
Map: OS Explorer 360

18

Loch Oude–Melfort–Loch Oude

Park in a lay-by on the east side of the A816, half way along Loch Oude, grid ref. 851159.

The **old coach road** ran from Lochgilphead to Oban. It descended to Melfort through the steep-sided ravine along which flowed the River Oude. When the high valley above the ravine was dammed the coach route was submerged. Towards the end of the walk look for traces of the track descending into the loch. Enjoy what remains of the track as you walk the route below the dam.

Old Coach Road

Peer over the old wall to see the bed of River Oude, which lost most of its water when the loch was created. Think of those travellers who made the arduous journey through the dark ravine—the Pass of Melfort. They were surely pleased to arrive at their destination and must have appreciated the A-road when it was constructed.

Primroses thrive along the sides of the ravine. In the mild climate of Argyll's west coast flowers appear in January often sharing hedgerows and banks with snowdrops. Here too the catkins on hazel trees lengthen and yellow in early January.

1. Walk on, south, from the parking area using the grassy verge. As you near the brow of the hill, cross the road with care. Go through a metal gate and descend shallow steps to the side of the dam. Pause on the

Walk 18

platform to look at the lichens, ferns, mosses, liverworts and the flowering plants that luxuriate in the dampness of the sheer sides of this dramatic gorge. Continue on down many more steps to join the old coach road. The way winds gently downwards, the towering cliffs on either side clothed with deciduous trees. When you reach a clearing in the woodland, look down across the tree tops to a fertile valley, with green slopes and hillocks beyond.

2. As you approach a gated junction with the A-road, take a path, right, just before a metalled road goes off in the same direction. Carry on along this delightful path as it descends through mixed woodland. Step across a stream and climb the slope ahead to join the narrow metalled road seen earlier. Turn right and continue on the pleasing way until you near the well screened Kilmelford hydro-electric power station, which makes use of the waters of Loch Oude. Here leave the road and take a track on the left that curves round right to cross the green painted metal bridge over the River Oude.

3. Beyond, turn right and walk ahead to pass to the right of the restaurant at the end of Melfort's timeshare complex. Go on, passing to the right of its laundry and in the direction of the power station, to a green signpost. Here bear sharp left in the direction of 'Fairy Hill and viewpoint'. The reinforced narrow track winds round and climbs below tall beech trees, keeping close to a blue water pipe until you reach several water tanks. The way then goes on up to a picnic table on Fairy Hill, a fine viewpoint. Continue on uphill, keeping left of a large hydro-electric pipe, which you finally cross to come to an open area and a small building. Here the huge pipe comes out of the hillside.

4. Stroll on along the continuing forest track, with spectacular views over the deciduous woodland in the very deep valley to your right. Look to the skyline to see the dam, passed earlier, strung across the narrow ravine. Enjoy the flaring cliffs tree-clad from top to bottom. Notice the dog lichen which grows in profusion among the grass of the forest ride. Ignore the first right—this leads down to where the hydro pipe emerges, again, from the hillside. Continue on the track to join another coming in on your left. Bear right, cross the burn and climb again on the other side of the valley. Then gradually descend the pleasing way, with the cliffs on either side seeming to tower higher and higher.

5. The track leads on beside Loch Oude. Dawdle alongside the pleasing sheet of water until you reach the end and then look down to see the old coach road descending into the water. Continue on to the A-road. Turn right to cross the road bridge over the River Oude. Just beyond, safely out of the way of the traffic, pause again to look at the tiny ravine through which the water flows into the loch. It supports a superb array of plants. Then walk on along the opposite grassy verge to return to the parking lay-by.

Practicals

Type of walk: This is a pleasing walk through dramatic scenery and fine mixed woodland. Walk this way when you wish to escape a gale. All paths and tracks are clear and pleasing to walk.

Distance: 4 miles/6.6km
Time: 2 ½ hours
Map: OS Explorer 359

Hen harriers

19

Luing Island

Park at the north end of the village of Cullipool, grid ref. 739132, where there is a large open area, with the sea on one side and huge riven cliffs on the other.

To reach **Luing** cross the Clachan Bridge to the reach the island of Seil. Continue to the south end, 4 ½ miles, following the signs for Cuan and the ferry. The latter plies every half hour and the return journey costs (at the time of writing) £5.50 per car and driver, and £1 for each passenger. The Sound is 200 yards wide and the trip takes 5 minutes. The ferry returns immediately to Seil. It is a dramatic waterway, with fierce eddies and swift currents. On landing, drive on for 2 ½ miles to Cullipool, the island's main village. Once slate quarrying was its main occupation. The ferry boat is named Belnahua, meaning Mouth of the Cave and is named after a tiny half mile square island off Cullipool. During the great slate boom around 150 people lived on the island, quarrying intensively except for the small area where the workers lived. Eventually the ravaged island was 'eaten' away and had to be abandoned early in the 20th century.

Cullipool, Luing

Hen harriers frequent the quiet moors, west of Achafolla, diligently quartering the marshy ground, with buoyant easy flight. They hunt for small mammals, frogs and insects, and the eggs and young of other birds. The male is pearly grey with black primaries, the grey on his belly shading into white. It is this distinctive colouring that makes him easy to spot. The larger female is a brown bird with a barred tail. Both male and female have white rumps and the flash of white when the female is in flight helps with identification.

Walk 19

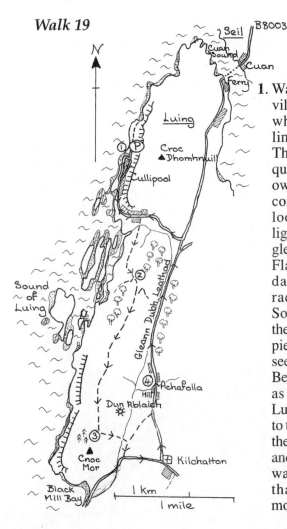

1. Walk back through the village where picturesque white washed cottages line the several streets. These were built by the quarry workers for their own occupation. As you come close to the shore look across to see two lighthouses, including the gleaming white tower of Fladda light, across the dangerous reefs and racing currents of the Sound of Luing. Notice the slate beaches and slate pier. From here you can see the deserted island of Belnahua. Follow the road as it winds left to pass Luing stores and continue to the end of the houses on the right. Here turn right and go through a gate to walk a reinforced track that runs out into moorland.

2. Take the first left turn along a track that climbs uphill. Near the brow carry on in the same southerly direction to go past a house and steading. From now on the track, rising and falling, passes through remote rolling countryside, from where you have good views across to Mull and, in the distance, of Colonsay. Ahead is the island of Scarba, a sprawling 1,500 foot high mountain, wild and inhospitable, composed of barren slate, except for a narrow strip of more fertile land on the east coast. Then Jura comes into view. As you begin to descend towards the large moss look, on the right, for a flat area bordered with a battered stone and turf dyke. Inside of the boundary you can see the ridges of old cultivation terraces.

3. Follow the track as it swings left at a stand of conifers and becomes a raised grassy causeway across the bog. At a cross of tracks, turn right and continue to the narrow road that runs through the centre of the island. Follow the road left and, at the crossroads, left again, to come to the old cemetery at Kilchatton. A notice warns you to take care as you visit the ruined church of St Cathan. Look for the gravestones close to the roofless building, including several elaborately carved stones. These were sculpted by the Covenanter, Alexander Campbell—he also dug his own grave. Continue on the very quiet narrow road for nearly half a mile. Look for the duck pond and sluice, on the right, and then, left, down a pretty ash-lined glen to the island's old mill. Its rusty waterwheel is still in place on the side of the red roofed building.

4. Continue past the school and on through Gleann Dubh Leathad, which means the glen of the dark slopes. The glen is believed to be inhabited by evil spirits but in spring, when the banks and slopes are softened with masses of primroses, evil spirits seem far away. Stroll on to the crossroads.

5. Turn left to walk back the short distance to Cullipool.

Practicals

Type of Walk: A lovely walk through a delightful island along quiet tracks and roads. Tremendous views.

Distance:	7 miles/11.4km
Time:	4 hours
Map:	OS Explorer 359

20

Easdale, Seil

Park by the pier at Ellanbeich, Seil, grid ref. 742174, or in the public car park behind the gift shop.

Ellanbeich is the principal village of Seil. It lies below the black slate cliffs of Dun Mor. The village was once a tiny island named, Eilean a'Beithich, or island of birches. It lay in a narrow channel between Seil and Easdale. During the 19th century, waste from the slate quarrying silted up the channel, uniting the two.

The tiny island of **Easdale** is separated from today's Ellanbeich by the narrow Easdale Sound. A small ferry—an open boat with an outboard motor—regularly crosses the sound. To call the ferry, if it is on the Easdale side, press two buttons in the shelter on the little pier; one triggers a klaxon and the other a light. The cost of the return trip, at the time of writing, is £1 per person.

Easdale is an island of slate except for a narrow high rock intrusion running through the centre. Its huge slate quarries were unrivalled and during the 19th century turned out nine million slates a year. In 1826 the harbours of Easdale and Eilean a'Beithich were constructed, together with the rows of workers cottages. During

Easdale and Ellanbeich

the night of November 23, 1881 a terrible storm arose, one of the worst that the west of Scotland had ever known. Huge waves swept over Easdale and at dawn the quarry holes of the island and of Eilean a'Beithich were flooded with sea water, making them unworkable.

Walk 20

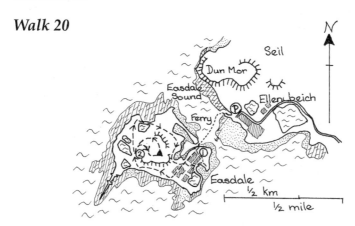

1. From the ferry landing walk through the narrow lanes lined with attractive white-washed cottages. More cottages edge two spacious greens. There are no cars or fumes and, apart from the breaking of the waves, the peace is delightful. Go on along a grassy path to start your walk round the shoreline of the island. Pass small outdoor sheds, roofed with huge slabs of slate. Look for gardens bounded by slates. Continue on in a clockwise direction to pass through a huge patch of low-growing, wind-cut blackthorn. To your right the ivy-clad geological intrusion of basalt, High Hill, with very obvious 'lava bombs', towers upward. Go on along narrow paths, on raised causeways of slate spoil, to pass between flooded quarries.

2. Close by two ruined roofless huts climb railed steps, which pass through heather and primrose Carry on up to the indicator panel on the summit of High Hill for a superb view. Notice the iron pyrites in the slate of the surround of the panel. Look down on the village to see the cottages and several more quarry holes filled with water, which is bright blue when the sun is shining. Then take another railed path that joins the upward path and comes down close beside the ruined huts once more. Go on round the island. Cross a long railed causeway between two more huge water-filled quarries—

here children need to be under tight control. Press on through large piles of slate waste. Wander into the village again and visit the museum set in the far corner of the largest green. Beyond the building, a narrow path takes you out to more quarry holes. Then dawdle back to the ferry.

Primroses

Practicals

Type of walk: Very short but extremely interesting. The still waters that fill the quarry holes are in great contrast to the white-topped waves crashing in on the little rocky island.

Distance: 1 mile/1.8km
Time: 1 hour
Map: OS Explorer 359

Clachan Bridge, Seil

21

The Island of Kerrera

The parking area, grid ref. 835283, has space for a dozen cars. It lies beside the Kerrera ferry slipway, two miles south of Oban, on a minor coast road, signposted 'Gallanach'.

In winter a small boat with an outboard motor takes five minutes to cross the **Sound of Kerrera**. In summer a slightly larger passenger ferry is used. Passengers on the mainland are asked to turn the board at the ferry slip to attract the attention of the ferryman at the advertised times. If the weather is doubtful check first with Oban Tourist Information Centre, tel. 01631 563122.

The island of Kerrera shelters the entrance to Oban Bay. It is a lovely green island, its unsurfaced roads used only by farm vehicles. It is wonderfully peaceful. Its fertile pastures support sheep and goats. It has fine cliff scenery and at the tiny Barr-nam-Boc Bay you can see the remains of the jetty where huge herds of cattle from Mull were landed on their way to market. The animals then walked the drove road to the east coast and swam the Sound to Oban.

Gylen Castle, perched high on a sheer cliff at the south-east end of the island, was built as a tower house in

Gylen Castle

1582 by Duncan MacDougall of Dunollie. It has a commanding view of the southern approach to the Sound of Kerrera and Oban Bay. It occupies a narrow promontory, access to which is by a vaulted passage under the main block. In 1647 it was burnt by Cromwellian troops. At the time of writing it is swathed in scaffolding and plastic sheeting is in place to shelter workmen who are stabilising the ruins. The project is going to take several years and is funded by the MacDougall, the clan and Historic Scotland.

Walk 21

1. Walk up the reinforced track from the ferry to pass a telephone box and a colourful kiosk that says 'Arts and Crafts and tea bothy'. Where the track divides, take the left branch and continue round the edge of Horseshoe Bay. Go on to pass the King's Field, a wide green pasture, where in 1249, Alexander II died on his way to visit Dunollie Castle. To the right of the track are high cliffs, where

cotoneaster and dark green ivy hug the sheer sides. Ignore the track, right, to Ardchoirc and go on ahead to wind round Little Horseshoe Bay. Follow the track until it winds right (1 ½ miles from the ferry) and here leave it and go ahead along a wide grassy track towards the sheep pens in front of the farm at Upper Gylen.

2. Turn left in front of the pens to go through a gate and on along a track, which curves right. It then levels out and becomes pleasingly grassy. Climb steadily through oak woodland until at the brow you can look down on an old farmhouse and outbuilding at Gylen Park. Just before it there is a small loch. Enjoy this delightful corner but do not descend to it. Instead bear right up a slope still on a distinct grassy path. Bear right and wind round left, with the path, to see Gylen Castle on its dramatic headland. Descend the winding path to come to the foot of the castle and then wander round the cliffs of conglomerate on which it stands. Look for the natural arch on the sea side. Go on round and then turn right to walk the narrow way to come to the fence protecting the stabilisation work.

3. Return along the narrow way and down a slope to the left to join a good track which winds just above the shore of Port a' Chasteil, Castle Bay, continuing under more spectacular conglomerate cliffs to come to a large grassy area. Here a large board directs you inland towards the bunk house and tea garden at Lower Gylen. This walk does not go that way but continues on to ford (bridge higher upstream) the burn that flows into Castle Bay. At the far side of the bay cross a rocky rib and descend to the right. Cross the next large green sward backed by similar cliffs and wind on round the bay to a gate. Beyond is the main track, which you join and walk left.

4. Head on along the way to pass, on the shore, a little cottage above Port Dubh. Continue on to pass a milepost, which tells you that you are three miles, in each direction, from the ferry. Pass in front of Ardmore house and follow the delightful way as it climbs steadily, contouring above Port Phadruig and passing a tiny lochan. Then descend towards a white house, at Barnabuck, picturesquely set in front of its backcloth of hills. Pause here to look back, to the left, to spot the remains of the once substantial jetty at Barr nam Boc. Pass the white house and then cross the bridge over a burn to start your way up the hairpins of the track. Watch out for a pleasing sighting of much of Mull, with Ben More in the distance. Then a little further on the view of the Firth is unobscured.

5. Continue on to pass another milepost. Look for the twin summits of Ben Cruachan overtopping the intervening hills. Carry on along the track as it descends through rolling pastures to a gate. Beyond, walk on and at the T-junction, turn right. The well made rough track goes on downhill. Go through a gate and follow the track to join your outer route, where you turn left. Pass the phone box and continue to the ferry.

Skylark

Practicals

Type of Walk: Choose a fine day for this delightful walk. Enjoy the freedom from traffic noise to listen to the island's birdsong, the wind in the trees and the sound of the sea.

Distance: 6 miles/9.8km
Time: 4 hours
Map: OS Explorer 359

22

Ganavan Bay and Dunstaffnage Castle

Park in the large car park at Ganavan Bay, grid ref. 863328. This lies two miles north of Oban and is well signposted.

The 13th century **Dunstaffnage Castle** was built by the MacDougalls, Lords of Lorne. In 1309 they were defeated by Robert the Bruce. Eventually he bestowed it on the Campbells, only for it to pass back again, peacefully, to the MacDougalls. In 1689 the castle came back into the hands of the Campbells. In

Chapel,
Dunstaffnage

1810, still a residence of the Campbells, it burnt down. It is a dramatic sight with its great stone curtain wall and its supporting towers built to conform to the huge irregular shaped 'lump' of conglomerate rock on which it stands. Considerable work has been done on the ruin to repair and consolidate it. It stands in a strategic position, commanding the junction of the Firth of Lorne with the Sound of Mull, and the entrance to Loch Etive. The extensive anchorage nearby made it doubly valuable.

Ganavan Bay has a long, wide sandy beach much enjoyed by families. From the bay there are spectacular views across the loch to Mull and Morven. Bird watchers will enjoy the gulls, oyster catchers, mergansers, shags and black guillemots.

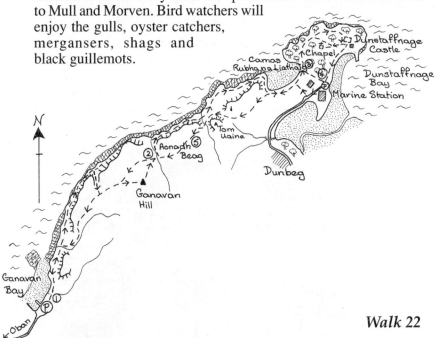

Walk 22

1. Leave from the far end of the car park and continue along the reinforced path to pass through a kissing gate. Continue on through shrubs to step over a small stream. Ignore the path to the right and go on along the clear, stony path below a magnificent conglomerate cliff. Out to sea you can view the southern tip of the island of Lismore. Continue until you reach a grassy gully rising steeply uphill before the next huge cliff. Ascend the path, on the left side of the breach in the cliffs. At the top, turn left to walk a clear track over the turf-capped cliffs. In a small dip three paths continue—

90

take the right one if you wish to climb Ganavan Hill for a magnificent view of the land and seascape. Go on from the top to descend to a fence.

2. Climb this and turn left to go down a narrow path to the shore. Bear right and walk the path below the dramatic cliffs. Continue along the pebbly shore for a short distance and then go on along the turf, following the good path that leads to a fence, with boulders on either side at the best place to climb over. Go on around the lower, but still fine cliffs to follow a path that leads down to a pebbly beach, Camas Rubha na Liathaig, from where you can see the marine biological station to your right. Continue over the turf just above the shore.

3. Step over the pipes that supply sea water to the marine station and stride a good grassy track that leads into scattered birch and sycamore, both covered with a variety of lichen. Follow the wide path

Black guillemot

through the trees, keeping parallel with the seashore. When you reach a widish track running inland, take this to come to the castle, which is obscured by trees until the last moment. To visit the castle continue to the ticket office beyond. Wander around the lovely site, go down to the modern day anchorage and then back to reach the gravelled access road. Almost immediately follow the signpost to visit the delightful tiny ruined chapel hidden among the trees. Here are the gravestones of many Campbells. Look for the two elegant window arches that remain almost intact. Then return to the access road and turn right.

4. Go through the castle entrance gate (or if closed bear right, then step over the inflow pipes before turning left at the end of a row of conifers). Pass to the right of the marine station and walk on to a stile on the right. Beyond, stroll on to wind left round the bay and then climb uphill to go through a farm gate. Follow the grassy track that tucks under a hillock to your right and, beyond, cross the field to go through another gate. Bear right towards the shore and wind round a small cliff. Here you are almost 'touching' your

outward route. Follow the indistinct path as it winds on and moves inland. Cross a stream and climb straight up a steep grassy hill. At the summit, pause for a superb view of the top of the castle and of the Connel Bridge.

5. Drop down on a clear path and up the next hill. Go down again to the first fence you climbed on your outward route. From here carry on ahead, with Ganavan Hill to your left . A short distance along, on your right, is the grassy gully you climbed near the outset of your walk and which you now ignore. The lovely rolling cliff top walk goes on and then when Ganavan Bay comes into sight the path, muddy at times, descends through gorse. Bear right to descend towards the shore. Step across the small stream and rejoin your outward path that leads to the kissing gate and the car park.

Dabchicks (Little grebes)

Practicals

Type of walk: A lovely walk for all the family. Choose a dry day because the stony path along the shoreline can be slippery. There is a path all along the shoreline, avoiding the 'diversion' above but, half way along there is a 'bad step' , with a deep crevice below, and most walkers will want to avoid this. Dogs are not allowed on this walk. The castle is open during the summer months (entrance charge).

Distance: 4 miles/6.4km
Time: 2–3 hours
Map: OS Explorer 359

23

Isle of Lismore— starting from North Point

The large car park at Port Appin, grid ref. 903454, lies above the ferry road, where there are toilets. The narrow road to the ferry jetty leaves the A828 south-east of Portnacroish.

The **ferry**, a small boat with a 12-seater cabin, takes about 10 minutes to cross the sometimes choppy Lynn of Lorn. It carries only passengers and bicycles It leaves Port Appin every hour and crosses to North Point on Lismore. The Caledonian MacBrayne Oban to Lismore car ferry takes 50 minutes but if you use this you will have to start this walk at point 5.

Lismore, Lios Mor in Gaelic, means Great Garden and that is just what it is. It is ten miles long and about a mile wide, with a narrow 'main' road from north to south. There are several side roads that lead over blowy hilltops and to sheltered bays from where there are marvellous views.

Castle Coeffin, Lismore

1. From the tiny slipway at North Point head on along the *Walk 23*
main road, with glorious views across the Lynn to the
mainland. Go on to pass below huge dark-grey limestone
cliffs. Below this scarp thrive ash, blackthorn, beech
and lime. On the shore side grow vast numbers of yellow
flags. Continue on for two miles and then take, on the
left, the metalled side road, signposted 'Balnure and
Broch'.

2. Follow the steadily descending road to pass, on
the left, Baileouchdarach farm. Head on for
nearly half a mile, towards the broch seen
clearly on its hill. Just before the road
swings right round a small hillock,
which hides Balnure farm, take the
metal gate on the left. Beyond,
follow a farm track for a short
distance and then wind left and
right to ascend the easiest way
to come to the side of the outer
wall of the mighty Pictish
broch. It is believed to have
been constructed sometime
after BC 500 and is named
Tirefour Castle on the OS
map. Wind round the
beautifully constructed wall
until you reach a gap into the
interior. Then, before beginning
your descent, pause and ponder
on the marvellous defensive position on which the broch was built.
Pause also to look down on little Eilean Dubh (Black Isle) and
then across the Lynn to Ben Nevis and Ben Cruachan. To the south
you can see the Paps of Jura.

3. Return to the road and continue on towards Balnure farm. Just
before its entrance, pass through the gate on the left, signposted
Balnagown. Stride on along the track to walk left of a derelict
farm. Beyond, climb gently between outcrops of rock. Go through
a breached wall and on through scattered gorse bushes. At the first
glimpse of Balnagown Loch, head right, downhill, towards a gate
beside the reed fringed pool. Carry on along the continuing track.

Go through a gate in the fence ahead and then stroll over a pasture to a gate in the wall, on your right. Press on with a pretty stream to your right and the wall to your left and then, where irises grow, cross over the water on a tractor bridge. Continue uphill to a signpost, where you meet the road.

4. Turn left and follow the road to descend to Mill House. Pass through a metal gate to a signpost. Here make a short diversion, bearing left, to look at the overshot mill wheel. Observe the warning not to enter the dangerous building. Return to the signpost and go on to a kissing gate. Stroll the continuing path to cross a small stream by a delightful clapper bridge, to stand in front of a very tall monument. This is dedicated to Waverley Arthur Cameron who drowned while sailing. Look back from here to see the broch and Black Isle. Go through two more kissing gates and then bear right to pass in front of a cottage and a house to come to the ferry road at Achnacroish.

5. Turn right and climb uphill. Bear right to pass Lismore primary school and the Historical Society Museum. Follow the road as it climbs gently over high pastures to join the main road. Turn right and walk on. Here in spring the banks are lined with primroses, wild garlic and bluebells. Go on to pass Lismore's shop and post office at Balliveolan. Stroll on for nearly a mile to take a track, on the left, signposted Castle Coeffin.

6. After 100 metres, look for an easy-to-miss small post, directing you left, leaving the track to continue beside a long drystone wall. Go through two gates to reach an arrowed post directing you on to another gate. Beyond, follow the clear track as it begins to descend. Look left for your first dramatic view of the gaunt ruin. Cross a shallow stream and then follow the track as it swings left. Here it becomes stony and starts its zig-zagging way down the steep

Yellow Iris

95

hillside to come beside the stream again. Follow this towards the magnificent ruin, the remains of a 13th century hall which stands on the site of a 11th century Viking stronghold. It towers upwards on the end of the high ridge above tiny Port a' Chaisteal. Return to the main road.

7. Walk left to come to the white-washed Lismore parish church of St Moluag, named after a contemporary of St Columba. Once the site was part of a much larger 14th century cathedral. Go inside to view its fine stained glass windows. Stroll on along the road to pass 'Moluag's Chair', a rocky outcrop and a fine viewpoint. Traditionally it is believed to be where the saint sat and meditated.

8. Continue on the main road for another mile to take the left turn to Port Ramsey. Walk the lane and on down to the shore and turn right to pass in front of a row of white-washed terraced cottages, which housed workers of the once flourishing limestone industry. Beyond the cottages carry on above the shore until you reach two very large limekilns. Just before them go through the gate, on the right, and take the track leading away from the shore. Follow it to a farmhouse. Bear right between the buildings. Carry on left, downhill to cross a wet area and then climb a little to join a clear track, where you turn left. Follow this below a wooded cliff and out into a grassy pasture. Curve right round the end of a hill, ignoring a gap ahead through the wall, and keep right (now beside the wall) until you come down to a gate above the main road. Join it and turn left to walk on for ½ mile to the ferry slipway.

Practicals

Type of walk: A long, rural walk through the northern half of a lovely island. Considerable walking along quiet narrow roads.

Distance: 11 miles/18km
Time: 5–6 hours
Map: OS Explorer 376

Glen Creran

Park in the small forestry commission car park, grid ref. 035488. To reach this take the A828 from Oban to Ballachulish. Turn off the main road at the bridge over Loch Creran to take a minor road along either side of the loch to its head. Then follow the very minor road which continues up the glen to Elleric.

Glenure was the home of Colin Campbell of Glenure who was shot in May 1752 near Ballachulish. This was known as the Appin Murder and found its way into *Kidnapped* by Robert Louis Stevenson. Colin Campbell was appointed by the George III to supervise one of the forfeited estates belonging to the rebels who failed at Culloden. Campbell was a vengeful man betraying anyone, acquaintances or friends, who had supported Prince Charles. He made many enemies who wished him dead. James of the Glen was hanged for his murder but no one in Appin believed he was the killer. In spite of a confession by someone else the courts gave him no reprieve and both confessor and James were hanged.

Glen Creran

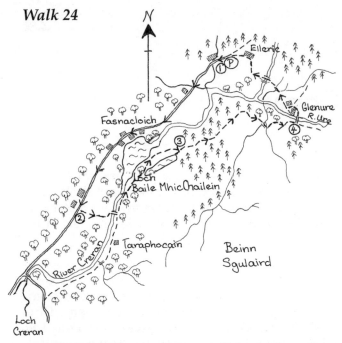

1. Turn left out of the car park to walk back along the road you have just driven. Pass a small church on the right, now converted into a dwelling. Continue along the pleasant lane with a good view out over Loch Baile Mhic Chailean to Beinn Sgulaird beyond.

2. After 2 miles/3.5km turn left down a track after passing first a telephone kiosk and then a large white painted hotel. Stride the track down across fields and follow it where it swings round to the left. Cross the River Creran on a wide wooden bridge, and turn left at the T-junction along another track, which runs beside the river. Look in spring for sandpipers bobbing at the waterside and swallows and martins skimming the surface after insects. Soon the river widens to become the reedy Loch Baile Mhic Chailein, and the path goes uphill and away from its edge. Another smaller loch appears on the right, so you are almost walking a causeway, with water on both sides.

3. Continue along the track as it winds downhill again and crosses an open boggy pasture to a forestry plantation. As you go enjoy the stunning views up Glen Creran. Pass through the gate at the start of the plantation and follow the track as it winds uphill. After a

short distance the trees on the right come to an end and the views are open again. Follow the track as it continues to climb and bends right towards the end of Beinn Sgulaird, which now towers steeply above you. Cross the bridge over a burn and then immediately ford another. Walk the track as it turns left to follow the lip of the ravine with the burns, now converged, below. Then swing right again, with an open woodland of mature scots pine and birch clothing the hillside to your right. Ahead Beinn Fionnlaidh looks rather lumpish and at the head of Glen Ure is the elegant cone of An Grianan, dominating the view.

Common sandpiper

4. Go through a gate in the deer fence ahead and turn left on the track coming down Glen Ure. A short distance along this track, cross the bridge over the River Ure, which here runs in a shallow gorge with beech trees. Turn left with the track and follow it as it goes down to the farm and house of Glenure, turning right towards animal pens. Just before the pens go through a gate, on the left, to walk in front of a whitewashed barn and house. Swing left across the pasture in front of the imposing Glenure House and turn right when you meet its tarred approach road. Go on through another gate and follow the road across pastures, where you might spot red deer. Cross the River Creran on one of the two bridges and continue on the road to Elleric. Pass between stone gateposts and turn left into the car park.

Practicals

Type of walk: A pleasing walk through quiet pastures, a plantation and beside a river, with magnificent scenery all around. Some road walking.

Distance: 5 miles/8km
Time: 2–3 hours
Map: OS Explorer 384/Landranger 50

25a

Bonawe Furnace

Park at Inverawe Smokery and Country Park, grid ref. 022317. This is reached by taking the A85 north east from Oban to Connel and then east on to Taynuilt. After crossing the Bridge of Awe, turn sharp left to drive the delightful narrow road for 1 ½ miles.

Bonawe Furnace was built in 1753 by a smelting company from the Lake District. It was in continuous operation until 1876. Iron ore was brought from the south to the site because here the charcoal for smelting could be provided in vast quantities. In the summer months the surrounding woods of oak and birch were coppiced and the charcoal produced was stored in the huge barns of the Furnace. The smelting took place during the winter. When production of the pig-iron was completed it was taken back south. The buildings that remain have been faithfully preserved by Historic Scotland and the site is well worth a visit.

Bonawe Furnace

Snowdrops

1. Leave the parking area and take the path signed 'Riverside Walk', which descends right, close beside the wall of the Smokery. Go through a gate and bear right to walk the path close beside the fence. This leads over a pasture to a superb suspension bridge across the River Awe. Cross and head up the pasture to a kissing gate in the top right corner. Turn right along the wide tree-lined track and continue on the pleasing way until just past Bonawe House, once the home of the Furnace manager. At the entrance gate to the house, ignore both left turns and go straight ahead on a downhill fenced track to turn left into the entrance to the Furnace at the bottom of the hill. Here wander at will to enjoy the excellent restoration.

2. Return to the car park by your outward route. As you cross the suspension bridge, look across the meadows to see fine Inverawe House.

See map on pages 102–103

Practicals

Type of walk: A short, pleasing level walk.

Distance: 2 miles/3.4km
Time: 1–2 hours
Map: OS Explorer 377

25b

Loch Etive

Park as for walk 25 a.

Connel Bridge spans the narrows between Loch Etive and waters beyond. The fine cantilever bridge was constructed in 1903 to carry the railway from Connel to Ballachulish, the line being closed in 1966. The bridge now carries the A828 to Ballachulish. Below are the Falls of Lora, often seen on the ebb tide. The unusual waterfall is caused by a ledge of hard rock at the foot of Loch Etive, which prevents the water dropping as fast as that of Loch Linnhe—to the west. When the tide returns the sea water races noisily over the lip of rock into Loch Etive. To see this phenomenon, stand on the turf viewpoint to the west side of the bridge.

The summer coat of **red deer** ranges from reddish-brown to golden-red. It changes to a brownish-grey in winter. Around and

Loch Etive

under the short tail is a patch of white and this is what alerts you to their presence—as they retreat—the white patch serving as a guide to other members of the herd when fleeing from a predator. The female bears her first calf at four years of age. From the end of May to mid-June she finds a lonely spot among bracken to drop her calf. It can stand within a few minutes of birth and can run within a few hours. It must be able to feed itself at four to five months. Deer live for about 20 years. They are browsers and grazers, those browsing on young shoots of trees and shrubs are heavy and form large antlers. Those who graze on grass are lighter in weight and have smaller antlers.

Walks 25a & b

1. From the car park, walk back along the approach road for a quarter of a mile and take a turning on the left. This well built road climbs uphill and then becomes a track, leading into the forest. At the Y-junction take the left branch to carry on through conifers. Ignore the left turn to Port na Mine and go on climbing steadily. Press on through more conifers. Eventually these are left behind and the waters of Loch Etive come into view seen through birch woodland. Stroll on along the forestry road, with the slopes of Ben Cruachan towering above.

2. Follow the track as it descends steadily, with stunning views ahead of Ben Starav and Beinn Trilleachan. Cross the wide Allt Criche, on a concrete bridge, as it rages down the slopes of the mountain above. Go on past a lonely bungalow and outbuildings. Stroll on quietly along the track as it winds right and climbs high above the River Noe. Here among birch and oak you might spot deer. Look

103

in the trees for long tailed tits making their presence known by their conspiratorial whisperings.

3. Cross the bridge over the racing river and wind right to come to the even more remote house and outbuildings of Glennoe, tucked in its hollow below the surrounding heights. Go quietly again in the hopes of spotting more deer high up on the slopes. This may be as far as you wish to go—three miles on a hard forestry track enhanced, for most of the way, with wonderful views of the loch and the mountains.

(If you wish to continue, the good track climbs on from Glennoe and winds round a headland. It passes above the remains of the deserted township of Creag Buidhe and then down to the River Liver. The way then moves a little more inland and crosses the River Kinglass to come to the sands of Ardmaddy. Beyond the route goes on as a path to the head of Loch Etive. At Coileitir you join a road and then cross the river by bridge [11 miles from Glennoe]. This road is reached from the top of Glencoe and if you wish to complete the 14 miles this would be the place to be picked up by a good friend.)

Pine marten

Practicals

Type of walk: A delightful ramble along a forest road beside magnificent Loch Etive. The views are superb, the quietness wonderful and the vegetation and wild life most rewarding. A very good walk for when a south-westerly is blowing hard.

Distance: 6–7 miles/10km
Time: 3–4 hours
Map: OS Explorer 377

104

26

Ben Cruachan

Park on the verge, in obvious parking places, opposite and to the east of the Power Station and Visitor Centre, grid ref. 079268. To reach the lay-by take the A85 from Oban to Taynuilt. Continue through the Pass of Brander with, to the right, an arm of Loch Awe. Do not use the visitor centre car park.

Ben Cruachan: A kilometer beneath the mountain is Scotland's green power station, a vast machine hall. Here electricity is generated by draining water from the Cruachan reservoir, through four huge turbines, to Loch Awe

W o o d w a r b l e r: The wood warbler, a s u m m e r r e s i d e n t, arrives late in the spring and departs before the

Summit of Ben Cruachan from Meall Cuanail

start of the autumn. It is a
yellowish-green bird with a
sulphur coloured breast and
throat. It delights in open
woodland of oak and beech. Its
song, a joy to hear, starts with
several loud throbbing notes
and ends with a silvery 'shiver'
as if a coin is being spun. The
warbler is often described as the
northern nightingale. Its nest is

Wood Warbler

C.M.Isherwood

usually found on the ground. A favourite place is on a bracken
slope where it is hidden by spreading fronds.

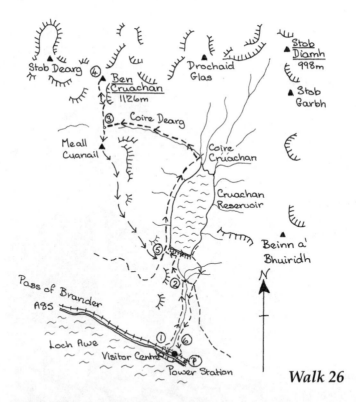

Walk 26

1. Take the narrow tarred entry road beside a slatted fence opposite
   the Power Station, just to the west (left) of the railway bridge over

the Falls of Cruachan. Follow the road up to the railway line, go through the small wicket gate and cross the line, obeying instructions to first look and listen. Go through the small gate opposite and immediately begin to climb, very steeply, through open birch and oak woodland where, in spring, violets and primroses carpet the woodland floor. Here you might hear willow and wood warblers and perhaps a cuckoo. You can also hear the falls off to the right hidden deep in the ravine. Follow the clear path as it zig-zags upward and then, where it levels off, emerge from the woodland. Cross the ladder stile over a deer fence and continue over boggy grassland to join a reservoir road.

2. Turn left and walk along the road to the foot of the dam, then ascend a flight of steps on the left, which takes you up to the overflow channel. Climb a ladder to a small gate, giving access to the top of dam. From the west end of the dam, turn left up a track and then almost immediately right to walk a good track, above the shore of the reservoir. Continue almost to the end of the track, where there is a cairn. Here go left to start your climb up Coire Dearg, soon to cross the burn and go up the far bank. Cross a number of side burns and continue climbing steeply to the head of the corrie to reach a col between Ben Cruachan and Meall Cuanail.

3. Bear right to begin your ascent of the ridge to the summit. The path is steep and scree-covered at first but it is easier on the right and avoids the worst of the scree. As you continue the paths proliferate among boulder fields and you will have to choose your own line. The angle is easier to the left, but take care not to go too far and get among crags. And then the summit is reached. It is small, neat and pointed and from it the views are superb. Look for Ben Nevis and the Glencoe mountains to the north, Mull and all the other islands south to Jura and even Arran to the west and south, and then Cowal, the Arrochar Alps and Ben Lui. Closer at hand you have views of the splendid mountain you are on, in particular the ridge leading to Stob Diamh, and the fine peak of Stob Dearg, the 'Taynuilt Peak'.

4. When you have enjoyed the panorama, retrace your steps to the col, where there is a small pool and a fence. Go up beside the fence, starting on the left and stepping over it from time to time, picking your own way up to reach Meall Cuanail. From here there is a fine view of Ben Cruachan and Stob Dearg. Continue down

*Yellow
Mountain Saxifrage*

the far side of Meall Cuanail on the close cropped grass to the left of the fence. Eventually you reach a plateau where the ground becomes boggier and the path veers away from the fence and disappears. At this point pick the best line you can, aiming for a point beyond the end of the dam, then wind your way down avoiding little crags, to join a good track. Turn left and follow this back to the dam.

5. Cross the dam and turn right at the end to stride a short distance down the reservoir access road. Look here, in spring, for yellow mountain and starry saxifrages on the cliff to your left. At a fork in the road, take the right branch and then go down the bank to pick up a path near the burn on the opposite side from the path you came up on. Cross a rather awkwardly angled ladderstile over the deer fence—if this defeats you at the end of a strenuous day there is a very large dog gate beside it which is much easier! Follow the path as it edges precariously above the ravine of the Allt Cruachan, descending through oak and birch.

6. Finally the path turns away from the gorge and crosses the hillside to an electricity installation. Take the steps going down beside this and go through a cattle creep under the railway line—the gate at the end does open in spite of appearances to the contrary. Go down steps to the road and return to your car.

Practicals

Type of walk: Very steep and very strenuous but most rewarding. The woods are a delight and the mountain scenery stunning.

Distance: 7 miles/11km
Time: 5–6 hours
Map: OS Explorer 377

108

27

Inveraray to Dun na Cuaiche (folly)

Park in The Avenue, Inveraray, grid ref. 095086. This wide road, with grassy flats and scattered trees on either side, lies beyond one of the archways to the north of the Information Centre.

Dun na Cuaiche is the high hill to the north of the village. On its delightful summit stands the 'watch tower' or folly, built for the Duke of Argyll, in 1748, by Roger Morris and William Adam. The hill has always been important to the Campbells because from it they could watch for intruders approaching through Glen Shira, Glen Aray and Glen Fyne. Before then its defensive potential had been recognised by earlier inhabitants of the area and on its flat top are traces of what might have been an iron age fort.

Inveraray is a pleasing small town on the north-west shore of Loch Fyne. In 1744, the Duke of Argyll decided to replace his ruinous old castle, which stood between the present castle and the sea. The old town of Inveraray was already three hundred years old by this time and it stood close to the old castle. It is reputed to have had 43 taverns. The Duke built his fine mansion and then needed the land around it to landscape his grounds. This meant that the town had to be moved to its present site. Plans were drawn up in 1753 and over the next 23 years new-town Inveraray gradually took

Tower on Dun na Cuaiche, Inveraray

shape. In 1776 the last of the houses in the old town were demolished and all traces of this flourishing Royal Burgh disappeared.

Walk 27

1. Just beyond where the A819 to Oban passes under one of the archways, take a left turn signed for the castle. Follow the tarred driveway as it bears right towards the pinnacled and turreted mansion. Look up to see the folly high on its hill, standing proud above steep slopes of deciduous trees. Follow the track past the castle and then on as it winds left to pass a memorial and guide post no.1. Cross the stately bridge over the River Aray. Continue on for a few steps to take, on the right, a narrow path climbing into woodland, past post 2. (Ignore the track that also turns right beside the river—your return route.) Leave the trees by a kissing gate, and cross a pasture to a gate directly ahead. Continue upwards on a track, passing through magnificent specimen trees, to pass post 3. After 280m look for post no.6, on your right, and here take the acute right turn. Almost immediately, turn left and begin a short steep climb up a narrow path to join a wide grassy track. Turn right and go on past no. 7. (If you do not like narrow steep paths carry straight on and follow the wide path to the summit.)

2. At no. 8 climb left up a flight of steps, with a rope handrail to help you maintain your balance. At the top of the steps the path makes a series of zig-zags as it continues ever upwards, and is generally railed with rope. Cross a rock fall (no rope) at no.10, with care, and pause to look down on Inveraray, sitting snugly alongside Loch Fyne. Go on up past no.

110

11 and then cross another rock fall. After a short rough stretch of track you come to a footbridge. Beyond, walk on to no. 12. Then climb a steep wet way to reach a clearing and the next post.

3. After walking through the long grass of the clearing you come to a track, where you turn left. Follow it as it curves upwards to the summit and where a stunning view awaits. Go into the folly and look down on Inveraray. There is a picnic table close to the folly and pleasing greensward for a pause.

4. Go back down the same track and remain on it, ignoring all other turns, including your path up. Soon it becomes reinforced and passes through conifers. In spring the way is lined with primroses, wood sorrel and golden saxifrage. Go round an acute bend to the left and carry on down. After descending for 700m look for the grassy left turn 30m before post no. 6 on your outward route. Continue along this, ignoring the path on the right and then the steps on the left, both taken earlier. Half a km beyond the latter, (past posts A-D) the level terrace path ends in a few steps down to a wide track. Turn left and look on the right for a narrow path and a post which has lost its label. Follow this path through an open area where there has been a vast clearance of rhododendrons. Enjoy the views as you descend steadily and easily to come to a picnic table on a wide track, from where you have a grand view of the castle.

5. Turn right and, as you walk, look up the steep slopes to the folly. Continue on with views over the meadows to Loch Fyne. Eventually you can see the River Aray through trees and then the track brings you to the road to the bridge crossed earlier. Turn left over the hurrying water and continue on the tarred road, past the castle and on to Inveraray.

Practicals

Type of walk: This is a challenging way to approach the summit and if you are not happy walking on a ledge-like path it would be better to use the wide track straight on from post no. 6.

Distance:	3 ½ miles/5.5km
Time:	3 hours
Map:	OS Explorer 363

28

Beinn Narnain and Beinn Ime

Park in the large car park on the shore of Loch Long opposite Arrochar, grid ref. 294049.

'**Arrochar Alps**' is the affectionate name given to the group of mountains that cluster around the head of Loch Long and the west side of Loch Lomond. They are readily accessible from Glasgow and were a favoured destination of early climbers who could use the train to get there. Beinn Ime is the highest, at 1011m, but easily the most spectacular is the Cobbler, at 881m, a Corbett, not a Munro. However to get to the top of the Cobbler requires scrambling ability and a good head for heights. Whilst there is some scrambling on Beinn Narnain, it is very easy and can mostly be avoided; it is a delightful rocky mountain and the views from it—particularly of the Cobbler—are outstanding.

The Cobbler from Beinn Narnain

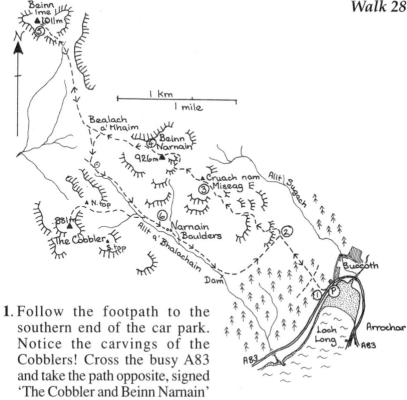

1. Follow the footpath to the
southern end of the car park.
Notice the carvings of the
Cobblers! Cross the busy A83
and take the path opposite, signed
'The Cobbler and Beinn Narnain'
and marked with a carving of a fox. The path leads into the forest.
It runs parallel with the road for about 30m and then turns abruptly
uphill. It follows a line of concrete blocks which formed the base
of a railway line used for carrying materials during the building of
the Loch Sloy dam. The occasionally eroded way then leaves the
tall trees and continues up through scrubby open forest with, in
summer and autumn, devil's-bit scabious and sneezewort lining
the path. Cross a forest track and scramble up the rocky bank at the
far side. Continue uphill, still following the concrete 'staircase'
for another 1km until the path emerges from the scrubby trees and
crosses a level grassy area on a low embankment. Here you might
spot grouse.

2. Ignore the path that goes off left (your return route) and carry on
upwards on an obvious but less good path. At a corner, scramble
up a low rocky face (or to avoid the scramble take a narrow path

113

looping round to the right). Go on over a boggy area and wind up the next slope. Most rocky outcrops can be avoided but if you enjoy a mild scramble they are quite easy! Then you arrive on the top of a little spur from where there is a stunning view of the Cobbler—one of the most amazing mountain skylines in Scotland.

3. Carry on upwards to the top of a ridge, Cruach nam Miseag, and there ahead is the Spearhead, the prow of Beinn Narnain's summit. Descend slightly to a col and then begin the final climb. The path winds round to the left and is somewhat exposed but easy to walk. Then it winds round right and crosses over below the Spearhead, through mossy boulders, with starry saxifrage and alpine lady's mantle. Ascend a gully on the right of Spearhead—it looks steep but is much easier than it looks. At the top you are on the summit plateau, which is rocky tundra, very level and pleasant. The trig point is neatly built of stones. The views are superb, especially Loch Long and Ben Lomond.

4. Beyond the trig point head towards a cairn. Continue downhill on a path in a westerly direction. Descend a short steep boulder slope to cross an easy grassy area. Then descend a steep path down the boggy Bealach a'Mhaim between Beinn Narnain and Beinn Ime. Cross the fence on the bealach by a stile and follow the obvious boggy path uphill, just west of north. Near the top, bear left, ford a burn and follow a drier path up through rocky outcrops. After levelling for a short distance, the path climbs to the neat summit, where the remains of a trig point and a big stone shelter sit on top of a huge rock.

5. Return by the same way (don't forget to turn right after crossing the burn.) At the Bealach a'Mhaim, cross the fence by the stile, once more. Bear slightly right, heading for the gap between Beinn Narnain and the Cobbler on an indistinct boggy path. Cross above a tiny lochan to the far side of the col where there is a more obvious path along the flank of the Cobbler; turn left on this and follow it down into the valley of the Allt a'Bhalachain (the Buttermilk Burn). This

Red grouse in heather

114

amazing high valley is full of huge boulders, with Beinn Narnain's rocky slopes towering on the left and the Cobbler's contorted skyline to the right. The path is rocky and boggy by turns but very clear and, where it joins the main path down from the Cobbler, becomes easier underfoot.

6. The path passes round two huge boulders, the Narnain Boulders, which give good shelter from rain and wind if needs be. Go on for 1km to a small dam across the burn. Here the path swings left and continues as a delightful terrace along the hillside, with Loch Long and the white houses of Arrochar below. All too soon this path comes to an end, at the corner where you left the main path on the ascent. Turn right and follow the concrete staircase back to the car park.

Sneezewort and Devil's bit Scabious

Practicals

Type of walk: Steep and quite rocky in places, and some wet areas. Both mountains are Munros and must be treated with respect—walking boots, full waterproofs, map, compass (and the ability to use it) are essential; but there are clear paths (some rough) all the way.

Distance: 8 miles/13km
Time: 6–7 hours
Map: OS Explorer 364

29

The Steeple and waterfalls on Donich Water, Lochgoilhead

Park in the loch side car park at Lochgoilhead, grid ref. 200012.

The village of **Lochgoilhead**, as its name describes, sits at the head of Loch Goil, a glorious sea loch and a branch of Loch Long. Easy access from Glasgow made it a favourite of wealthy Victorians and here they built their houses. The tree-hung shores are accessible by road only at two points: Carrick midway along the western shore, and the village at the head of the loch. Between the two is a road alongside the loch. North of the village the road climbs to over 700ft (213m) providing fine views of Lochs Long and Fyne.

In spring the leaves of the **bluebell,** or wild hyacinth, break through the soil and lie close to the ground in a rosette, leaving a circular tube through which the flower bud arises. Before the plant has finished flowering the leaves are a third of a metre in length and by this time the flower stalk is twice as long as the leaves. The

Waterfalls, Donich Water

flower head droops delicately but becomes erect when the three-celled capsule develops, full of ripening seeds. Then each cell splits, releasing the shiny black seeds.

Walk 29

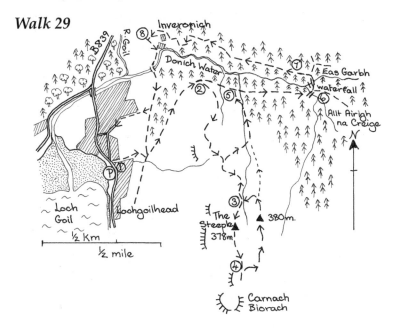

1. From the nearby telephone boxes cross the road and follow the footpath sign to continue up a track. Pass the public toilets and carry on the now narrow way, with the houses soon left behind. Climb the stile beside a gate and turn sharp left to climb beside the fence on your left. Ignore the next gate but a little further up go over the fence by another stile and then through the kissing gate beside it. Turn left to climb the good forestry track, with mixed woodland on the left over which towers Ben Donich. To the right flowering gorse clothes the slopes. Continue on to pass, on the left, a fine stand of scots pine.

2. A short distance on along the track from the pines take, on the right, a track that climbs the slopes, plainly marked by tractor wheels. Press on up the rather wet but easy way to walk to the first brow. Follow the tractor trail as it winds and curves round the outcrops, passing through bracken and heather, and finding the easiest way. Soon the bracken is left behind and there is heather all

around. Continue ascending until you can see The Steeple (390m) ahead.

3. Leave the well delineated route as it continues through a narrow glen on the left side of The Steeple and begin your ascent (right) to the little summit. The view is superb and if the weather is kindly you will want to linger. All around are high hills, not quite Munros or Corbetts but tall craggy tops. Down below is Loch Goil with the tiny picturesque village hugging the shore. Beyond high hills to the north you can see the Cobbler with Beinn Narnain beyond. After enjoying the top go on to descend, pausing to look back at The Steeple's fine prow of schist. Drop down steadily to the tractor trail through the glen between The Steeple and Carnach Biorach.

4. Join the tractor trail and follow it as it swings left. Leave it very soon to bear left to walk along the lovely heather-clad ridge, now looking across the glen to the summit of The Steeple. Stroll on to the high point and then, if you feel comfortable finding your way across trackless slopes, begin your steady descent, slightly right, picking your way carefully along grassy patches between the long stalked heather. Avoid any sudden tiny precipices and head towards the trees of the forestry plantation to your right. If you decide this is not for you, then, from the high point, descend bearing left, with care, to the highest part of the glen between you and The Steeple. Here turn right to follow the tractor trail, following any one of several tracks. Whichever route you take, go on down, keeping on the left of the plantation to return to the forestry track once more.

Bluebells

5. Turn right and at the gate, take the stile on the left to carry on along a glorious rocky path. It descends through fine mixed woodland, with the noise of the tumbling Donich Water away to your left. Press on to where, in an idyllic corner under trees, the water of the Eas Garbh and the Allt Airigh na Creige come together to form the Donich Water after descending in a magnificent waterfall and sparkling cascades.

6. Cross the first footbridge and then go ahead on the forest trail, ignoring the track that goes off right, the old hill path to Coilessan Glen and on to Ardgarten on Loch Long. Climb the stepped way to cross the high level bridge over the deep chasm worn by the mountain stream, before it plummets in the superb waterfall. Head up the stepped way to a track, where you turn left.

7. The delightful descent through the bluebell woodland seems to go on forever. Regularly through gaps in the trees you have stunning glimpses of the loch and the mountains on its western side. Carry on down, with Stob na Boine Druim-fhinn straight ahead. At the foot of the path, join a wider track and bear right.

8. Follow the way as it swings left below a towering fir with, to your right, a fence and sheep pastures beyond. To the left is Inveronich farm. Cross the Donich Water on a good bridge. Wind left and then right on the track to come beside, on the left, the forest again. Continue on to take the wide track on your right. This leads through a delightful grassy picnic area and then on to the road, opposite the fire station. Cross and walk left into the village.

Practicals

Type of walk: A great walk of contrasts. The unrelenting climb to The Steeple is over heather moorland, following tractor trails. The descent can be equally challenging. The second part, to see the waterfalls, involves a little climbing and then a long descent on good tracks and through pleasing woodland. You may wish to make the ramble into two walks.

Distance: 4 miles/6.5km
Time: 3–4 hours
Map: OS Explorer 363

30

Ardentinny to Carrick Castle, Cowal

Park at the Forest Enterprise car park near Shepherd's Point, north of Ardentinny, grid ref. 191885, where Glen Finart meets Loch Long.

Carrick Castle dominates the scenery along the west side of Loch Goil. The castle is a 14th century, three storey tower house, built on a rocky promontory by the side of the loch. Additions were added in the 16th century and it was used by James IV as a hunting lodge while a guest of the Campbells. In 1685 the castle was burned to punish the Campbells who had supported the Duke of Monmouth's rebellion against King James VII.

This is a **walk** of two parts. The first half is easy—an initial climb through the forest, followed by two miles along an easy-to-walk forest road. The second half is much more challenging, especially after rain when the path, under dense conifers, can be muddy and the tree roots slippery. The descent to the bridge over

Carrick Castle

the Allt Reinain can also be wet. Once over the Allt Reinain bridge and down a dry path, you need to head for the shoreline to avoid one of the wettest areas in Cowal! The return is along the same route and this must be allowed for in terms of daylight and energy. If you find this too daunting you could make use of Pete McNab's taxi for the return from the castle to where you have parked. It is a long way round by road and at the time of writing the fare was £20—but it is a glorious ride. There are Stagecoach Western buses and you will need at least two to return. For information tel 01369 707701

Carrick Castle

Castle

Ardnahein

Loch Goil

Allt Reinain

Rubha nan Eoin

Walk 30

1 km

1 mile

power line

Pylons

Knap

Loch Long

N

Stronvochlan

Shepherd's Point

Finart Bay

Ardentinny

1. Leave from the far end of the car park, cross the burn and climb all the steps. Follow the path as it winds round a gully and then on along a spur. Carry on the path where it unexpectedly winds left and goes on up. Join the forest road and turn right. Here in birches on the left you might spot bullfinches. The track descends steadily with a fine view across Loch Long to Coulport. The latter has a huge steel building believed to have been used for handling explosives used in nuclear submarines. Continue on along the way. Look out to the sea loch, where you might see eiders, seals, oyster catchers, shags, mergansers and goldeneye. Stroll on with the water of the loch lapping the shore to your right. To the left where large areas have been cleared of conifers, grasses, bracken, silver birch and moss have pleasingly colonised the slopes.

2. Go on along the track, sometimes close to the shoreline of the loch and sometimes high above it, to pass between conifers—the haunt of red deer. Follow the track as it winds and climbs and passes between tree-clad rock faces. Continue winding left, uphill, to pass an enormous pylon on your left. Go on up until you come to a second pylon at the end of the track.

3. Here return a short distance to take a narrow indistinct unmarked path, now on your left, up a slope, with tall larch to your right and a tiny burn to your left. Continue on ahead over churned up ground, keeping along the edge of the unfelled trees. Soon you reach a tiny plank bridge over a stream—the first of many—and you know you are on the right of way. The path goes on, now deep into the forest, crossing seven more plank bridges before reaching a marker post. Beyond you begin to descend gently along a ride between sitka spruce. Cross a small burn on boulders.

4. Emerge eventually from the conifers into pleasing birch woodland from where you can look down on Loch Goil. Then descend on a clear path (muddy after rain) and continue to the Allt Reinain to cross on a fine footbridge. Go quietly here as you might see red squirrels. Once over the bridge, climb the slope to go over a stile and continue down towards a fence, beyond which is a pasture. At an easy-to miss waymark climb the fence using a convenient stone on either side and continue towards the shore.

5. Bear left along the shingle and sometimes over slippery rocks to continue on to where a small stream emerges. Find your own way on along the shore, winding round a shingle point and along a rocky causeway. Then head

Red squirrel

up a pasture to a waymarked stile over the fence, with houses to your right. Go on the clearly waymarked route, behind the dwellings and then Ardnahein farm. The track leads round right to come to the road. Turn left and walk on to Carrick Castle, with an impressive view up to Lochgoilhead. Return by the same way.

Bullfinches

Practicals

Type of walk: An interesting walk full of contrast, best done in the summer or after a dry spell. After prolonged rain it becomes a much more challenging trek.

Distance: 5 miles/8km—one way
Time: 2–3 hours—one way
Map: OS Explorer 363

31

Glenbranter, Cowal

Park in the Forest Enterprise car park above the houses in Glenbranter village, grid ref 112978. Glenbranter is three miles south of Strachur and the car park is clearly signposted off the A815 between Strachur and Dunoon.

Glenbranter was the forestry commission's first acquisition in Scotland. In 1921 it bought 10,000 acres of the estate belonging to Sir Harry Lauder, the renowned musical hall artist. He had intended that the estate should provide for his beloved son John when he returned from the 1914–18 war. But in 1917, Captain John Lauder of the Argyll and Sutherland Highlanders was killed in action. After this tragedy Sir Harry and his wife could not bear to remain at Glenbranter and they moved to Dunoon. The car

Waterfall, Glenbranter

park stands close to the site of Glenbranter House.

Mosses, liverworts and lichen carpet the boulders, ground and many of the tree trunks in the glen. One very obvious grey-green lichen, which festoons the branches of trees, is nicknamed Old Man's Beard because it does look beard-like as it grows in tufts or tassel-like masses. *Usnea subfloridana*, its Latin name, is the commonest and most widespread species in Britain and it is restricted to areas with little or no air pollution.

1. Three walks start from the car park, the routes delineated by posts with coloured bands. This walk to the waterfalls in the glen follows posts with yellow bands and the outline of a footprint. Leave the car park at the opposite end from which you entered and almost immediately, at the Y-junction, take the right branch to climb a raised causeway through glorious deciduous woodland. Join a forest track and bear left. After a short distance look for the waymarked left turn to continue along a high-level terraced way. This leads to a narrow path descending through magnificent trees and a variety of rhododendrons. Here in spring, where light filters through the trees, primroses, bluebells, foxgloves and wood sorrel flower. In the damper areas rushes, sedges and ferns thrive. Listen as you walk, for cuckoos, woodpeckers and many small songbirds. Go quietly and you might come upon roe deer and red squirrels.

2. Go on descending to join a wider track, where you turn right. Carry on through conifers. Beyond, press on to descend steps to a viewpoint, then bear right, following the yellow banded posts. Cross a footbridge over a stream and go on the railed way to pass a fine waterfall. Wind steadily left around the head of the gorge. Go up steps to the foot of another pleasing fall, then cross it by a footbridge.

125

Walk on to see the main fall on the Allt Robuic. Here the burn descends furiously into a turbulent plunge pool and then goes on down the gorge in a series of white-topped cascades.

3. Descend steps, wind round left and follow the hurrying burn back down the gorge. Cross a bridge over the Allt Robuic and climb up to follow the path along the opposite bank. Pause to look across the glen to the waterfalls seen earlier. Go past some sculpted trolls and then through open mature forest to take a long row of steps, bringing you to a forest road. Here turn left to cross the Allt Robuic again.

4. Just beyond the bridge, turn right along a narrow path through a fine plantation of well spaced sitka spruce, with moss and grass between the scattered boulders of the forest floor. These trees were planted in 1926. Look as you go for deer tracks along the path. Follow the way as it comes to the edge of the burn and then winds left. It eventually brings you to the forest road once more. Turn right to carry on past the stone houses of Glenbranter. Just after the large white house on the left, turn left to walk a good track. Very soon take the track going off right, another delightful way below an avenue of redwoods. Climb the slope to return to the car park.

Old Man's Beard lichen

Practicals

Type of walk: A short walk along forest paths and tracks leading into a deep gorge with spectacular waterfalls. Children should be under firm control.

Distance:	2 miles/3.4km
Time:	1–2 hours
Map:	OS Explorer 363

32

Linear walk alongside Loch Eck

Park in the well signposted Forest Enterprise car park at Glenbranter, grid ref 112978. (See walk 31).

Lovely **Loch Eck**, very long and narrow, stretches, ribbon-like, almost from Loch Fyne to Loch Long. Its deep, dark waters pleasingly reflect the mountainous, tree-clad slopes that run steeply down for most of its lengthy eastern and western shoreline. In its cold waters thrives the rare powan, a freshwater fish rather like a herring. It also lives in shoals. It became trapped after the loch was cut off from the sea during the last ice-age, 10,000 years ago. Along the loch's 8-mile west side is a virtually traffic-free track, delightful for walking at any time of the year. The east side is traversed by the A815.

The **Benmore** estate was given to the nation in 1925 by the Younger family, associated with Younger's beers. A few years later,

Loch Eck

as Benmore Botanic Gardens, it became an outstation for Edinburgh's Royal Botanic Garden. It has a wonderfully varied collection of conifers and rhododendrons and several well signed trails. It also has a plant and gift shop, and a good restaurant sited on the edge of the car park

Walk 32

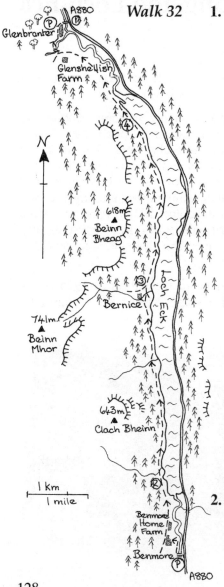

1. Return from Glenbranter car park to the A815 to pick up a Western bus (484, 476 or 486) which will take you, south, along the eastern shore of Loch Eck. Alight at the Benmore Botanic Gardens and Outdoor Centre car park. Walk right of the shop and the restaurant and then follow the road, left, to pass below an avenue of enormous redwoods. Cross an ornate bridge over the River Eachaig and turn right. The tarmacked way winds left and climbs towards several fine buildings, one of which is a grand clocktower. At the T-junction beyond, turn right in the direction of Bernice. Continue on to pass, on your right, Benmore Home farm. Stronchullin Hill rises upwards on the opposite side of the loch. Ahead is a stunning view of the loch, with ridge after ridge of mountain slopes descending, on both sides, towards the water. Carry on to a gate at the end of the reinforced way.

2. Climb the stile to the left of the gate and press on along the continuing track, enjoying the reflections in the water and the

huge boulders covered with moss and lichen, which litter the steep hillside. Climb the next stile, beside a gate, and carry on. At the T-junction wind right, ignoring the turn to Bernice outdoor centre, a charming white-washed house. Climb the next stile and, a short distance beyond, is a left turn, which you also ignore. This is the track up into Bernice Glen. The name Bernice is derived from Bearnais, the Gaelic for gap, and high up on the mountain slope is a dramatic gap. It was through this that the Campbells travelled, quickly and safely, across this part of Argyll. Look for golden eagles here.

3. Continue on the delightful way, climbing through conifers and then descending again with satisfying glimpses of the loch. Again the track climbs and there are very steep slopes down to the water, so sheer that you wonder how the foresters could have kept their balance when planting.

Immature golden eagle

4. At the T-junction, take the right branch to descend steadily. Proceed on along the head of the loch where many bushes and shrubs thrive in the fan of rich alluvial soil deposited by the River Cur long ago. Ignore the left turn and press on to pass Glenshellish farm. Follow the track as it winds right to cross the bridge over Glen Shellish burn. Beyond, turn left and then immediately right, up the yellow banded way. In a few steps take the right turn to walk the excellent path beneath an avenue of redwoods. Climb the slope to reach the car park or head on to the A815 to pick up a bus.

Practicals

Type of walk: This is a glorious stroll beside one of Argyll's most delightful lochs. It is easy to walk with very few slopes to climb. The views are stunning. It is an excellent walk for a cold or wet day and beautiful when the sun shines.

Distance: 8 miles/13km
Time: 3–4 hours
Map: OS Explorer 363

33

Puck's Glen, Cowal

Park in the car park at the Younger Botanic Garden, grid ref 143856, this lies on the west side of the A815.

Puck's Glen is one of Cowal's secret gems. Through the glen is a waymarked path, originally constructed by the Younger family, (the Edinburgh brewing dynasty and former owners of the Benmore Estate) to lead to a folly on the hill, now reconstructed in the Botanic Garden. The path follows a natural gorge, with dramatic overhanging cliffs and a series of roaring waterfalls. It passes through mixed woodland planted by the estate in 1870. It has the wonderful wild, romantic atmosphere so much enjoyed by the Victorians. For many years the paths were neglected and unsafe but in the mid-1980s they were repaired by the Forestry Commission, with the assistance of the Manpower Services Commission, who put in steps, new bridges and drainage ditches.

The uncommon **filmy fern,** *Hymenophyllum,* is a delicate feathery plant that

Waterfall,
Puck's Glen

luxuriates in the perpetual mist of the waterfall and the continual run off of water down the steep slopes.

Filmy fern

Walk 33

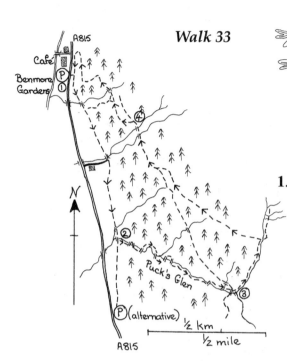

1. Cross the road with care and go towards the sign that says Black Gates Road. Bear right to continue along the old road that runs parallel with the A815, where you pass under magnificent redwoods and silver firs. Enjoy this quiet way which is well surfaced and suitable for wheelchair visitors. Where the road swings right, go ahead, following the sign for the glen. Cross the bridge over the Eas Mor (Big Fall) by an old milestone, which reads 'Dunoon Pier 6 miles'.

2. Turn into the forest through a kissing gate and go down steps to the side of the burn, deep in its dark tree-lined gorge. Walk upstream on the good path, crossing several footbridges and winding round a huge rock bluff down which descends a fine waterfall. The path goes on up, crosses another bridge and curves round beside another spectacular fall. Go on to pass through a man-made gap in a huge boulder, with the burn squeezed into a narrow canyon. At the signpost, ignore the right turn and continue up the glen, crossing more footbridges. Here the rock sides of the gorge flare upwards

131

and support tall trees and the sky is a pale blue oblong even higher. Just before the next waterfall look for the uncommon filmy fern on the wet rocks beside you. Cross the burn and climb steps beside another fall, seething angrily where it is imprisoned by the gorge. Then two lots of railed steps take you high above the raging water, to reach the forest road.

3. Cross and go on up the upper glen on narrow paths and steep steps beside the burn. Continue past a water chute, where the water foams wildly. At a board across the path, with written instructions for those continuing over the hill, turn acute left, following the signboard for Black Gates. Cross a boggy area by moving in and out of the trees. Then the path rapidly improves and it gently descends and passes through conifers. At the forest road, turn right in the direction of Black Gates. Carry on until you have passed a large quarry face and then a tumbling stream, hurrying through a narrow, steep-sided gorge.

4. Just beyond, turn left into deciduous woodland. Go on gently down and look for the board directing you to a viewpoint. Pause here to see Glen Massan, with high mountains on either side. At the Y-junction, ignore the left turn and go ahead on a level narrow path to join a track coming uphill on the left. Continue on where it winds and then bends back again and comes to a fallen silver fir. Climb the steps to a platform on the top of its trunk to read the interesting facts on a board. Continue on down to join your outward path and cross the road to the car park.

Practicals

Type of walk: A steepish dramatic walk on a good path through the lower glen. The upper glen, hard by the burn, is an exciting walk in the gloom among great fallen trees, many of them brought down in earlier gales. All the family will enjoy this adventurous trail but children must be under close control.

Distance: 2 ½ miles/4km
Time: 2 hours
Map: OS Explorer 363

34

Linear walk: Ardnadam to the Bishop's Glen, Cowal

Use the car park on the sea side of Pier Esplanade, just south of Dunoon Pier, grid ref. 176764.

Dunoon lies on the west side of the Firth of Clyde. It can be reached by car and pedestrian ferry from Gourock. Once it was a popular resort for the teeming day-trippers and holiday makers from Glasgow. The 19th century saw it favoured by the city's wealthy business men and entrepreneurs who built their second homes in Dunoon. Today it is a quieter pleasant place where visitors like to stroll its long breezy promenade and browse in its good range of shops. Once outside the town you very soon find quiet single-track roads, with only the scenery of the long, indented, stunning coastline to distract you. Take care if you are driving!

Burn, Ardnadam Glen

Siskins are as acrobatic as tits and hang upside down when picking at alder cones or birch seeds. In spring they seek out insects and insect eggs on a variety of trees. The tiny striking male is olive-green, darkest on the back and shading to yellow on the rump, the female is browner and striped, and much less easy to spot.

Walk 34

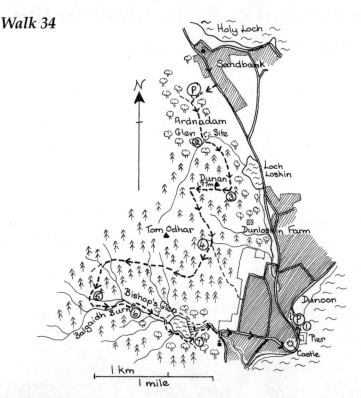

1. From the car park, walk a few yards, south, to the Ferry Terminal to take a Western bus (484, 485, 476, 486) towards the village of Sandbank—a 9 minute journey. Alight opposite the Primary School and take the track, going off left and signed 'Ardnadam Glen'. Go through a kissing gate and turn left to walk into delightful oak and hazel woodland, where you might spot long tailed tits and siskins. The path continues through lush ferns, clumps of juniper and sweet gale, to come to the Ardnadam Enclosure. Turn left to read the information board that suggests this site has been occupied for over 5,000 years. Look for the low stone wall foundations of a single storeyed chapel still surviving after 1,000 years. Look also

134

for the sites of several roundhouses, marked by white posts, and the dyke around the enclosure, all of which may have been constructed by Iron Age farmers 2,000 years ago.

2. After your exploration, return to the main path and swing right to cross the burn on a footbridge. Continue up the steps to cross another bridge and then go up more steps to stroll on through the glorious woodland. Pause at a seat to look down on a hut platform believed to be the site of a timber roundhouse. At the cross of paths, turn right to pass another hut platform and follow the track as it climbs steadily. Below, through the trees to the left you can glimpse Loch Loskin. Carry on along a ride between conifers and then emerge from the trees to come to another seat from where you can look down on Dunoon and the Firth of Clyde.

3. Just beyond the seat, look for the right turn to start your climb up Dunan (177m). The name means 'little fort' in Gaelic and that is what it probably was. The distinct way climbs quite steeply to the summit cairn from where there are outstanding views of the Clyde and Holy Loch. It is believed that the latter was given its name after a ship, carrying soil from the Holy Land to be used for the footings of Glasgow Cathedral, sank in the loch. To continue the walk, go on down the other side of the hill and carry on up a good track through low conifers. Alas, it soon deteriorates into a muddy way churned up by mountain bikes. It climbs steadily to join a high-level forest track, where you swing left and descend for about a kilometre, through sitka spruce, to a T-junction.

4. Turn right and begin climbing through more spruce to a seat, from where there is another superb view. Continue climbing for another kilometre and then follow the way as it begins to descend. Here look for a cairn, on the left, at the edge of a grassy 'lay-by'. This is opposite a wooden bridge and steps. Bear left here on the easy-to-miss delightful path that descends through larch and carpets of heather into Bishop's Glen. Follow the distinct path to the side of a tributary of Balgaidh Burn, which you cross on stones. Beyond, follow the clear path as it winds left.

Siskin

135

5. Pick your way carefully as you progress along the sometimes wet and winding path, following where other walkers have trodden through this magical corner of the glen. For a short distance the burn, now to your left, descends far down in its valley. Eventually the path brings you near to the edge of the hurrying water and you wind right to come to a small clearing and the Balgaidh Burn. Pause here to locate the best way to cross and notice where the path climbs the banking and goes on. Press on through scrub and under trees to come down to a bridge over the main burn, which you cross.

6. Bear right along duckboarding to reach a reinforced track. Stroll on through birch to a seat from where you can enjoy the burn descending in a delightful waterfall. Then take the steps on the right. Ignore the bridge over on the right and continue on the main path. Cross the next bridge over the burn, where it flows into a picturesque reservoir. Wind left to continue with the sheet of water to your left. Then cross a bridge over a narrow dramatic gorge and climb the steps through woodland.

7. Head on along the track and take the left branch, downhill, at the foot of the reservoir. Do not cross the bridge below the dam, but keep on the same track with the stream far down below, on the left. Ignore the next bridge and walk on. Then cross the next bridge, where the burn descends in great tumult, and carry on to a gate to the road. There is a fine stone bridge and a church to the right. Bear slightly left and then descend Auchamore Road and the continuing Tom A'Mhoid Road to the Esplanade.

Practicals

Type of walk: This is a very pleasing and sometimes challenging walk through mixed woodland, high above Dunoon, from where there are some superb views. The route passes fascinating sites of Cowal's ancient past. It uses good tracks and footpaths and, after heavy rain, some wet ways.

Distance: 5 ½ miles/8.8km
Time: 3 hours
Map: OS Explorer 363

Glendaruel, Cowal

To reach the parking area, grid ref. 995842, take the narrow road off the A886 for Clachan of Glendaruel. Turn left beyond the hotel and park in a lay-by, on the left, just before the entrance to the churchyard.

Clachan of Glendaruel is a small township with a fine hotel, a splendid church, ancient grave slabs, a few pretty cottages and houses, and toilets. Kilmodan Church dates largely from 1783 and is a grand mix of Presbyterian simplicity and Georgian elegance. It is the third to be built on the site. Look up on the front wall to see the coat of arms of Sir Dugald Campbell, with the date 1643, taken from an earlier church. St Modan was a Celtic saint living at the same time as St Columba.

In a small building, a lapidarium, in the churchyard is a fine collection of carved **grave slabs**, dating from the 14th and 15th centuries, and probably sculpted by a group of stone carvers who travelled from place to place wherever they were needed. Around the year 1110 a band of Vikings passed through Glendaruel and were slaughtered.

1. Return from the church and turn right to pass in front of Glendaruel Hotel. Continue to the A886 and, with care, walk right. After 200m leave the A-road to turn right along a narrow road, signed 'Otter Ferry' and go on to cross the River Ruel on a fine bridge built by Thomas Telford. Carry

Grave Slab, Glendaruel

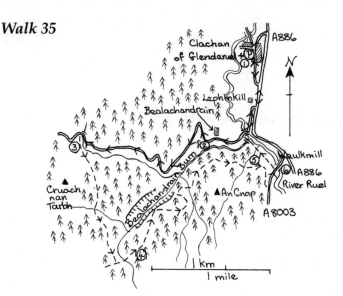

on along the delightful lane. Notice the collapsed bridge on your left and decide whether you will be able to cross it towards the end of your walk. If not, observe the instructions given at the end of this walk. Maybe it has been repaired by the time you walk this way or, of course, it might have completely collapsed. Follow the lane to pass the access track to Bealachandrain farm.

2. Then begin the long climb up the pass, where tall oaks, ash and sycamore clothe the very steep slopes down to the sides of the Bealachandrain burn. Follow the road as it swings left and levels for a short distance. Pause here to look down on the farm to see the outbuildings forming an enclosed courtyard behind the house. Carry on up through birch and conifers, where you might see bullfinches. Look left, across a clearing in the forest to a superb waterfall. Stroll on up to reach the summit of the pass, where the road swings round a shallow valley filled with boggy rough pasture.

3. Here take a wide green track, leading off left, to a gate which stands directly below a power line that marches across this high point. Climb the fence beside the gate to walk on along an old forest track, which soon leads into the conifers. In places the way can be muddy and lined with rushes but it is very clear to follow. Look for fox droppings and the footprints of both red and roe deer. Go quietly and you might see the deer crossing the path ahead. On either side of the way goldcrests and coal tits whisper in the trees. Press on as the track climbs gently to join a rough stretch of forest road, where you turn left.

4. The way climbs first and then begins to descend and soon the surface becomes much more walker-friendly. Pause at the viewpoint to look down on Glendaruel. Move left, with great care, to look into the huge gorge that cuts through the forest Through it flows the Bealachandrain burn, descending in a series of dramatic waterfalls. Here on convenient boulders you might wish to take your midday break. As you continue to descend the surface becomes a joy to walk. Carry on through a delightful glen, where deciduous trees line a small burn.

5. Go on down and down between lush banks carpeted with mosses, lichens, ferns and shrubs. Then the winding track comes to a locked gate, with a gap for walkers to go round beside the gatepost, to join the A8003. Turn left and walk the quiet way to come beside the River Ruel.

6. Here you must decide on your return route. If you do not wish to cross the collapsed bridge, go over the next road bridge and continue to join the A886, where you turn left to walk for nearly 1.5km to take the left turn for Glendaruel. If you are happy to cross the collapsed bridge, turn left before the road bridge along a 'no through road'. Go round a barrier and walk on the pleasing grassy way, with the river to your right. Continue on to cross the damaged bridge, wriggling through a narrow gap at either end to rejoin your outward route. Turn right, and walk on to cross the Telford Bridge. Complete the 200m stretch along the A-road and then turn left to return to Glendaruel.

Practicals

Type of walk: The ascent of the marvellously engineered pass is steep but full of interest. The route has been in existence since 1769. The return through the forest is a quiet delight.

Distance: 6 ½ miles/10.5km
Time: 3 hours
Map: OS Explorer 362

36

Tighnabruaich–
The Pheasantry, Cowal

Park in the well signposted car park, facing the sea, in the small village of Tighnabruaich, grid ref. 983731.

Tighnabruaich looks across the Kyles (narrows) to the island of Bute. It is a pretty village and has shops, hotels, a youth hostel and a marine boatyard to cater for holiday makers. It has many fine, colour-washed villas, with delightful gardens that run down to the shore road. These were built in the last century, as country retreats, by Glasgow's wealthy entrepreneurs and business men. Steep hillsides tower up behind the pleasant village, their slopes clad in mixed woodland, much of it infested with rhododendrons— a beautiful sight in spring but creating many problems for the owners of the forest and sometimes for walkers. From the village there are stunning views of the island of Arran.

Kyles of Bute. These narrow sea inlets separate Bute from the mainland. The claw-shaped land of Cowal seems to hold the island in its pincers. The

Lighthouse at the Pheasantry, Tighnabruaich

mudflats of the mainland, exposed at low tide, teem with bird life. At the right time of the year look for oystercatchers, curlews, goldeneye, mallards, herons, mergansers and eiders.

1. Cross the road from the car park and walk left along the shore road to its end. Carry on the continuing track to pass through a boatyard. Then take the railed way, which rises up from the shoreline alongside a huge cliff of convoluted schist. This supports heather, wood sage and pennywort. Follow the way as it descends and winds

Walk 36

½ km

½ mile

N

waterfall

Creag Rubha Bhain

Tighnabruaich

A8003

Pier

P

A8003

The Pheasantry

Eilean Dubh

disused lighthouse

Kyles of Bute

West Glen

Rubha Ban

round Rubha Ban. Continue on the lovely track, with sheltering slopes to the left covered in lush vegetation, including the ever-present rhododendrons. As you near a Y-junction, look through a gap in the larch on the shore side of the track to see the Maids of Bute— two small rocks, painted in garish colours for clothes—across the Kyle.

2. Take the left branch to climb into the Caladh Plantation above West Glen house and cottages. Cross a bridge over a hurrying waterfall and stroll the level track and go on where it descends. Head on along the pleasing way towards the Pheasantry and its charming disused lighthouse. It is pepperpot-shaped, stands proud on its tiny isthmus and is very white against a background of Scots pine. Follow on along the track as it winds inland to come level with the garages of a stone house.

3. Here turn left, off the main track, and climb steps and the continuing narrow path that keeps parallel with a stream. This brings you to two waymarked posts, with green tops and discs. Ignore the one to the right and follow the other, left. This directs you across a turf bridge over the stream. Stroll the delightful way, high up in the deciduous woodland, where you might spot roe deer or their footprints. Head on down to come parallel with a fence on your left. At this point the path is muddy after rain and indistinct and the waymarks, at the time of writing, have disappeared. But if in doubt, press on, parallel with the fence and then heading uphill and diverging slightly from the boundary, pass under rhododendrons. Then the waymarks start again and you can spot the lighthouse far below.

4. The path now widens and its surface improves as it continues uphill to cross a tiny stone bridge. Go on by an unexpected gracious waterlily pond and then make a short descent. Bear left with the path and then, in a few steps, ignore the track continuing downhill and bear right, crossing a stream—a favourite haunt of roe deer. Climb steadily, negotiating several fallen trees and passing under a neck-height, telephone cable. Go on through conifers, where the sun slants delectably through the trees. Follow the distinct path

Sparrowhawk

through mixed woodland, avoiding the cable once more. Notice the vast amount work that has been done to remove the rhododendrons. Keep a watchful eye for red squirrels and great spotted woodpeckers. Progress with care where the cable runs along the path.

5. On reaching a forest track, turn left to descend to your outward route, where there has been much work on clearing the tiresome bushes. Turn right, cross the bridge over the waterfall and, after descending, turn right along the shore track. Continue to Tighnabruaich.

Eiders

Practicals

Type of walk: This is a magical walk, glorious on the outward route and delightful on the return through the forest. The final stretch back to Tighnabruaich gives you a second chance to enjoy the superb views, particularly the distant mountains of Arran and Holy Island.

Distance: 5 ¼ miles/8.5km
Time: 2–3 hours
Map: OS Explorer 362

37

Portavadie, Cowal

Park in the Forestry Commission's Glenan Walk car park, grid ref. 929698, off the road to the ferry at Portavadie. "Wee Geoff's" buses run to Portavadie (Tarbert ferry) from Dunoon on four days a week, tel 01700 811473. Stagecoach Western buses run to Portavadie from Dunoon twice weekly, tel 01369 707701.

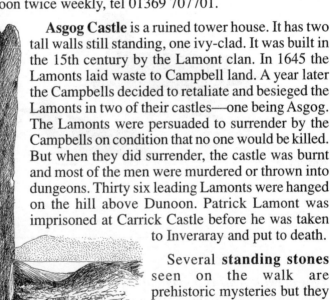

Asgog Castle is a ruined tower house. It has two tall walls still standing, one ivy-clad. It was built in the 15th century by the Lamont clan. In 1645 the Lamonts laid waste to Campbell land. A year later the Campbells decided to retaliate and besieged the Lamonts in two of their castles—one being Asgog. The Lamonts were persuaded to surrender by the Campbells on condition that no one would be killed. But when they did surrender, the castle was burnt and most of the men were murdered or thrown into dungeons. Thirty six leading Lamonts were hanged on the hill above Dunoon. Patrick Lamont was imprisoned at Carrick Castle before he was taken to Inveraray and put to death.

Several **standing stones** seen on the walk are prehistoric mysteries but they do indicate a settled population. It is suggested that they might have been used in relation to the cycle of the moon, helping farmers to time when to plant their crops.

Standing Stones, Stillaig

The concrete village of **Pollphail** was built to house workers who were to build concrete platforms for drilling oil. The area was chosen because it had access to very deep water. A huge hole was excavated for a dry dock. Alas, oil drilling was taking place far away on the east coast of Scotland and the drillers wanted steel not concrete platforms. This brought about the failure of the government funded scheme because the site failed to obtain any orders. Now the large number of buildings are deserted. They have decayed steadily over the years leaving an eerie, ugly, silent sprawl.

Walk 37

1. From the parking area walk back to the road to the ferry and turn left. Carry on and turn left again, at the sign for Asgog, to ascend an aggressively red forest road. This soon moves into deciduous woodland where you might spot bullfinches. Look ahead to see a white house. Where the track swings left towards the house, go ahead along a path through bracken, following a roughly painted direction sign. Follow the waymarkers, orange-topped posts, as the path climbs to come close to the white house, now on the left. Here, after crossing a small burn wind right and go on up into the forest. The lovely way passes through an open area and then on through denser woodland. At the next open area you can glimpse the sea, far down through larches.

2. Go along the path as it begins to descend through bracken, with fine views of the hills ahead. Continue where the hillside has been cleared of trees and left to regenerate naturally. Then you have your first glimpse of Loch Asgog. Follow the path as it winds down to the ruined castle, with several pretty cottages to its right. Stroll on along

145

the continuing wide grassy track through bracken, with the loch to the right. Climb the stile to the right of a gate and go on through gorse. On reaching the pasture, keep well up above a boggy area and go ahead to a turf bridge through a wizened hawthorn hedge.

3. Head up the slope to a gate gap in a fence and pause to enjoy the superb view of Arran and its mountains. Then carry on downhill on a cart track to the road. Turn right and walk to the Millhouse crossroads. Turn right along the signed road for Tarbert ferry and Portavadie. Climb steadily uphill along the road, which is quiet unless the ferry has just arrived! Loch Fyne soon comes into view, with Tarbert on the far side and Kintyre beyond. You can also see Stillaig farm away to the left and, beyond it, more of Arran. Descend steadily and then up again to come to a seat—perhaps your picnic spot.

4. Carry on a for a few metres and then turn left into a wide track. Look for reed buntings in the bushes close by a damp area. Press on up the track and then wind down in the direction of the sea. As you go, look right to see the first fine standing stone. Then look from here, across the moorland, to see another on the skyline. Go on down the track to come, unexpectedly in this remote corner, upon two large huts belonging to the boys' brigade. Continue ahead over a grassy isthmus onto a small island, Eilean Aoidhe. Walk right and climb a narrow path that soon leads down to a rocky bay. Here aspens grow high up in the sheltered gullies of the schist cliff face. Here too you might spot stonechats on the rocks, festooned with ivy, above the aspen. Pause awhile to enjoy the singing of the seals and to enjoy the lovely view of the little island, Sgat Mor and its lighthouse, with Arran beyond.

5. Return towards the two large buildings and turn left along a narrow path through bracken to come to a raised area, encircled with stones. This is all that remains of a bronze-age burial cairn. As you leave the cairn, take a few steps towards the shore to pick up a grassy path where you walk right through bracken. This brings you to a tiny burn with a causeway on the far side—Port Leathan. Upstream is a footbridge over the burn but it is unsafe and you should cross at the easiest point, nearer to the sea. Once across, go on upstream to the far side of the bridge

Reed bunting

to join a narrow path, reinforced with old bits of wood. Follow it through rushes and purple moorgrass and then go on along the footpath, through rhododendrons, to come to a cottage, with a grassy vehicle track leading to it.

6. Turn right along this track, away from the cottage, and walk past a ruined croft. Go on to the corner of a turf-walled enclosure, where you should turn left and strike up an indistinct path over grass and through bracken. Away to your left you can see several ruined crofts. Keep to the sea side as you wind round a hillock. Then look ahead to see the standing stone, viewed earlier from across the moorland. Narrow paths and sheep trods take you down a gully and then through heather moorland to pass through a turf wall. Beyond, stands the 3m high stone and just before it a short, stubby one. It is more difficult from here to spot the earlier standing stone. Pause here to enjoy this emotive spot, high on wild pastures above the sea.

7. Walk on along a narrow path in the direction of Portavadie, passing through another turf dyke, and keeping high above a dumped rusting lorry. Wind right of a rocky outcrop and go on over heather moorland. Descend the path through birch woodland, and then scrubby gorse, to reach a broken fence. Pass through and drop down to cross a dry gully onto a concrete track. Turn left and walk along this beside the eerie, gaunt buildings of Pollphail village. Follow the concrete track to pass through a gap beside a gate and then on to join the road. Turn right and almost immediately left to walk the ferry road. Continue until within sight of the terminal. Then turn right to return to the parking area.

Practicals

Type of walk: A glorious route at first through mixed woodland. It continues by a pretty loch overlooked by a ruined castle. Eventually the way passes a standing stone and then goes on to a tiny island. The return is over pleasant moorland, still in sight of the sea, to come to two more standing stones—a magical trail.

Distance: 7 ½ miles/12km
Time: 4 hours
Map: OS Explorer 362

38

Kilmichael, Isle of Bute

Park at Glecknabae, grid ref. 005682. To reach this drive north from Rothesay on the A844 to Kames Bay and follow the A-road as it winds left, inland. At the Y-junction take the B875 to Ettrick and go on, north west, along the continuing narrow shore road to where it ends in a pleasing parking area.

Many men must have been needed to carry up the huge slabs of stone, which lined the burial chamber of **Glenvoidean Cairn**. It is not known whether this mausoleum of a Stone Age chieftain was built as protection against evil spirits or to contain the souls of the dead. More porticos and chambers were added over the following centuries.

Glenvoidean Chambered Cairn, Bute

Kilmichael, or St Michael's chapel, is dedicated to the Irish saint, Macaille. The picturesque ruin stands on a grassy sloping sward overlooking Kames and Tighnabruaich on Cowal. Families from these two townships were brought across the water to be buried in the churchyard surrounding the chapel. One lovely legend tells of a shepherd's dog who, after his master was buried in the churchyard, swam across the Kyle and was found lying beside his master's grave.

1. Walk on from the car park along a track through glorious woodland, where you are likely to see roe deer. After about 1km, turn left to walk down to a shingly beach. Continue scrambling easily over rocks to a tiny inlet from where a ferry once ran across the Kyles of Bute to Kames and Tighnabruaich. Return to the track and then cross, left, to a collection of rocks prominent in the middle of a pasture. This is St Michael's Grave, remnants of a Neolithic chambered cairn and named after the nearby chapel. Continue on across the pasture to go through a gate in the wall and then strike slightly left across the next pasture to the gate in the wall ahead. Bear left across the third pasture, to pass through an old iron gate to visit the precincts of the ruined chapel.

Walk 38

Kilmichael

½ km

½ mile

St. Michael's Chapel

③ Glenvoidean Chambered Cairn

Old Ferry Port

Michael's Grave Chambered Cairn

Woods of Lenihuline

Kyles of Bute

Glecknaboe

2. To return go through the iron gate and then right to pass through the gate taken earlier. Turn left and walk to a gate on to the track, just in front of a pretty cottage. Turn left for a few steps and then take a rising track turning acute right to a farm gate. Just beyond, climb up a path, on the left. Very soon you can spot two slabs of stone, forming a V and pointing upwards from amidst a large clump of vigorous gorse. Head right to join the farm track and go on up to the second hairpin bend to

come to the Glenvoidean Cairn on the left. Wind round the bushes and the stones to find the entrance, the only part still free of the invasive bush.

3. Return down to the main track and turn left to pass the cottage and stride on return to the car park. Turn right here to take a small path through the trees to a seat by the shore from where you have a glorious view across the Kyles. Here you might spot the gannets, eiders, oystercatchers and mergansers.

Roe deer

Practicals

Type of walk: A delightful stroll on a good track to see several of Bute's ancient sites. The way up to the Glenvoidean Cairn can be very muddy.

Distance: 3 ½ miles/5.8km
Time: 1–2 hours
Map: OS Explorer 362

39

Barone Hill, Isle of Bute

Park at the west end of the causeway that dams Loch Fad, grid ref. 078625. To reach this, leave Rothesay by the B881. Just after the castle, branch right along the B878 (Russell Street), following the fish-shaped signs, with Loch Fad printed on them. After half a mile take a narrow left turn, signed Loch Fad, where, after a mile, you reach a three-way split of roads and tracks. Take the left fork for the parking area, which lies just before the causeway.

Barone Hill (162m) is a panoramic viewpoint from where you can see much of Bute. Look across the Firth of Clyde to the mainland and then west to see the dramatic skyline of Arran with, beyond, a glimpse of the peninsula of Kintyre. The large flat summit, with its trig point and rough low walled shelter, was the site of an ancient fort. It also gave refuge to the people of Rothesay when, in 1334, the town was attacked by Edward Balliol intent on recovering the Scottish throne given to his father, John Balliol, by Edward I.

Standing stone, Craigbiorach

Loch Fad, two miles long and a quarter of a mile wide, lies in a trench caused by the Highland Boundary Fault, which is a split in the earth's crust. The Fault goes right across Scotland to Stonehaven, though it isn't a trench all the way. On Bute this fault separates the northern end of the island, composed of schists, from the southern end of red sandstone and slates. The causeway or dam retaining Loch Fad was built in the 18th century. In 1818 Robert Thom, a water engineer raised its height as part of a scheme for supplying more water power to the cotton mills in the town.

1. From the parking area walk back along the approach route to the three-way split of tracks. Here take the second left turn, ignoring the first, which is a private road to Woodend House. Climb the metalled way to pass through large stands of conifers. Continue until you leave the trees behind and then descend to a gate. Beyond, stride ahead, ignoring the road as it goes on left to the water board buildings. Ascend the

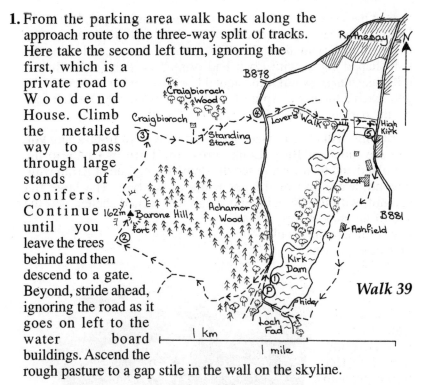

Walk 39

rough pasture to a gap stile in the wall on the skyline.

2. Turn right and climb beside the wall to reach the pleasing airy summit where you will want to pause to enjoy the magnificent view. Go on down beside the wall for a short distance until the indistinct path drifts away from it, winding easily around outcrops and mire. It descends quite steeply to a plank bridge and then a stile in the fence at the foot of the hill. Walk ahead up the pasture, keeping beside the fence on your right, to pass through a gate onto a track.

152

3. Bear right and walk on along the way that could be muddy after rain. Where the track turns left towards a derelict farm, pass through a scrubby hedge and strike, half left, towards a fine standing stone. Beyond, follow a grassy gap between the tall gorse bushes to come to the side of walled Craigbiorach Wood. Turn right to walk to the kissing gate at the end of the woodland. Once through the gate go on across the pasture, bearing a little left, to find a track through the encroaching gorse bushes—beautiful when in bloom. Go on downhill and continue beside the wall on your right to come to a gate to a narrow lane.

4. Walk left and, in a few steps, take a right turn to carry on along Lovers' Walk. Dawdle under trees beside a tiny flower-edged stream. This is one of several 'water cuts' made by Robert Thom, which fed extra water into Loch Fad and Kirk Dam—another lower reservoir, now with much less water and surrounded by encroaching reeds. Where the track winds left continue ahead to cross a wooden bridge. Then climb steps to a small stone gateway into High Kirk Cemetery. Spend some time here looking at the fascinating headstones. See if you can find Robert Thom's. Leave by the gates onto the A881

5. Ascend steadily right and then, just after the primary school, bear right to walk a track that leads towards Loch Fad. Before you cross the causeway you might wish to visit the bird hide that looks out over Kirk Dam, where you might spot heron, tufted duck, coot, mallard, little grebe, teal and wigeon. Cross the causeway to return to the parking area.

Practicals

Type of walk: A walk of contrasts—a fine hill climb with dramatic views from the summit, a pretty path beside a 'cut', a bird hide and an extensive loch to visit. Fine views of Arran.

Distance: 3 miles/5km
Time: 2–3 hours
Map: OS Explorer 362

40

St Blane's and Glencallum Bay, Bute

Park at the end of Plan Road, grid ref. 093531, where there is a small parking area.

In the 6th century a Celtic monastery was believed to be established by St Catan on higher ground, above the present day Plan farm. The ruin, **St Blane's**, takes its name from St Catan's nephew, Blane. The rectangular building within the lower burial ground, the fragmentary remains of cells along the foot of the cliff and the enclosure wall probably date from this period. It is believed that the monastery was destroyed towards the end of the eighth century by the Vikings. The medieval church and the upper burial ground possess fine twelfth century workmanship. The view from the site is delightful and the parkland and fine trees make this a tranquil atmospheric corner, where you will want to wander.

St Catan's sister became pregnant by an unknown man. She and her new born child, Blane, were cast adrift in an oarless coracle

St Blane's Chapel

by the enraged Catan. The boat was eventually driven ashore on the coast of Ireland. Blane was taken in and educated by the monks of the nearby monastery. He then travelled through Europe but in time returned to Catan's monastery where he was reunited with his uncle. Later he succeeded Catan as abbot of the monastery and bishop of the area. In time Blane, known as the mild, moved east to Pictland. It is here that he is remembered, particularly for his foundation beside the Allan Water, which was to become Dunblane Cathedral.

1. Go through the kissing gate onto the access track to the farm. Immediately go through another kissing gate on the left and ascend the gently rising pasture. Cross a stile and turn left into the precincts of the St Blane's chapel, where there are several explanatory plaques which will help you enjoy your explorations. Go through a metal gate to reach the chapel. The site eventually became deserted and was taken over by Norse incomers. Look beside the fine remains of the chapel for the hogback tombstone

Walk 40

which covered the grave of a Viking settler. Leave by the metal gate and swing right to pass through a wall gap, then right again to a gate onto a track, where you turn left. Climb steadily to a green sward, with gorse all about, to come to a gate and stile. From here there is a dramatic view down to the sands of Stravanan Bay.

155

2. Strike half right, downhill to go through a gate. Then climb beside the fence to your right. Continue ascending, up and up, to where the fence turns right. Follow it for a few metres and then strike, left, straight up the lower slopes of Suidhe Chatain (Hill of Catan). Press on up to a stile in the fence and then over the wall beyond and carry on up to the trig point. From here there are superb views of Kilchattan Bay, the Cumbrae Islands and Arran.

3. Here a choice has to be made, either to continue and then descend a rather steepish path, or, to return to where the fence turned right and go on ahead to pass through a gate. Turn left to descend a steep well marked path, parallel with the wall on the left, to a wicket gate in the wall. Beyond, descend to the back of some houses and then through a gap to reach the shore road. For those who do not wish to turn back, press on over the top and begin your descent. The narrow path takes you down and down to a flatter area. Follow the path as it continues ahead into woodland and winds round several fallen trees before it begins to swing sharp left, still winding through trees. It then climbs a little bank and descends an old track. Turn right at the bottom. On reaching the track behind the houses, turn right to walk below the steep wooded slopes you have just avoided by bearing left. When you reach a gap between houses turn left and cross the shore road. Walk right along the green sward with several seats from where to enjoy the pleasing view over the sea. Look for Kiln Villas on the other side of the road and notice the enormous limekiln set back behind the dwelling.

4. Just beyond the villas take the old track that climbs right. The way winds right and then sharply left but take the short cut, on the left, across the loop. Then continue left along the track. Just before a gate into woodland, turn right up a tractor track that first winds right and then goes on upwards. It then bears left above a large clump of gorse to a waymark on the skyline. Carry on ahead with a pretty reservoir to your right and the skimpy remains of the once strategically sited Kelspoke Castle, to your left. Continue to the stile at the end of the reservoir.

Hare

156

5. Press on along the wide green sward to begin your gradual descent to a stile. Follow the waymarks, left, through a derelict wall then the path that goes on down to a signpost on the grass of a wave cut platform, just above the sea. Look back to see the dramatic sandstone cliff, Hawk's Nib, a fantastic rock formation sculpted by wave action. Turn right to walk below the towering cliffs. Look and listen for eiders just off shore. The shore path, a little rocky at times, brings you to a grassy area, with the lighthouse away to the left. Wind round right to come to Glencallum Bay, another place where you will want to idle.

6. Continue to the far side of the bay and then follow the path that climbs steeply right. Go on along it as it begins to turn left to a waymark. Carry on left to walk the lovely high level way, with superb views down to the sea. Continue to the next waymark, on the skyline, and stroll on. As you go, look right, down to a loch. This is pretty Loch na Leighe, which is the way this walk continues. To reach the pleasing pool, go on a short distance and then follow a clear path, right and downhill, to walk along the left side of the loch.

7. Stroll on along a wide grassy trod with low hillocks on either side. As you near the farm observe the waymarks directing you right across two footbridges and then left onto a path that soon winds right to join a good track. After a few metres, turn left and climb the slope signed, 'St Blane's and the West Island Way'. The little path teeters along the edge of a steepish drop to the farm. Carry on the airy way to climb a tall ladderstile. Walk on with a wall on the right and with St Blane's now in view. Go on to the stile just below the site. Turn left and descend to the parking area.

Practicals

Type of walk: An exhilarating walk, with ancient ruins, a good hill climb and descent, and a sea shore walk below magnificent cliffs.

Distance: 4 ½ miles/7.4km
Time: 3 hours
Map: OS Explorer 362

Clan Walks

A series of walks described by Mary Welsh, covering some of the most popular holiday areas in the Scottish Highlands and Islands.

Titles published so far include:

1. 44 WALKS ON THE ISLE OF ARRAN
2. WALKS ON THE ISLE OF SKYE
3. WALKS IN WESTER ROSS
4. WALKS IN PERTHSHIRE
5. WALKS IN THE WESTERN ISLES
6. WALKS IN ORKNEY
7. WALKS ON SHETLAND
8. WALKS ON ISLAY
9. WALKS ON CANNA, RUM, EIGG & MUCK
10. WALKS ON TIREE, COLL, COLONSAY AND A TASTE OF MULL
11. WALKS IN DUMFRIES AND GALLOWAY
12. WALKS IN ARGYLL AND BUTE

OTHER TITLES IN PREPARATION

Books in this series can be ordered through booksellers anywhere. In the event of difficulty write to:
Clan Books, The Cross, DOUNE, FK16 6BE, Scotland.